ALSO BY CALVIN TRILLIN

Family Man

CALVIN TRILLIN

Family Man

FARRAR • STRAUS • GIROUX • NEW YORK

Farrar, Straus and Giroux
19 Union Square West, New York 10003

First edition, 1998

Library of Congress Cataloging-in-Publication Data
Trillin, Calvin.
    Family man / Calvin Trillin. — 1st ed.
        p.   cm.
    ISBN 0-374-15324-8
    1. Trillin, Calvin—Family—Humor.   2. Authors, American—20th
century—Family relationships—Humor.   3. Child rearing—Humor.
I. Title.
PS3570.R5Z467   1998
814'.54—dc21
[B]

*Some passages in this book originally
appeared, in different form, in* The New Yorker
and other magazines.

For Alice

Family Man

1

No Advice Here

Handing out advice on family matters is not my game. When I'm asked by new parents for tips on child rearing—this happens regularly to anyone whose children have managed to grow up without doing any jail time—I've usually said, "Try to get one that doesn't spit up. Otherwise, you're on your own." I find myself with even less to offer when approached by young people in search of wisdom about how they might go about linking up with someone with whom they are likely to enjoy a long and happy marriage. (According to what I've read in the newspapers, long term marriage is making a mild comeback, after a number of years during which, as I noted in the eighties, it was inextricably intertwined in the public mind with the music of Lawrence Welk.) It's true that my wife, Alice, and I have been married since Lyndon B. Johnson roamed the halls of the White House, and it's also true that the police do not regularly stop at our house for what is sometimes known in the trade as a domestic disturbance beef. But I think that young seekers of guidance would be disappointed if I revealed to them what, in retrospect, is the only strategy I can divine from what passed for my wife-seeking activities thirty-odd years ago: "Wander into the right party."

If I had any family advice I was confident of beyond those maxims, I suspect I would be inclined to keep it to myself. When our older daughter, Abigail, was four years old, she attended a progressive nursery school in lower Manhattan that was sweet and nurturing and, if I may say so, a little bit earnest. It was the sort of place where teachers would say to a kid who had just attacked another kid, "Use words not hands, dear." (At one point, we all began to wonder exactly what the words for sneaking up behind another kid and pulling her hair might be. All I could think of was something like "I'm a nasty little beast who deserves a good hiding.") This was in the early seventies, and any number of new ways of looking at American society were beginning to coalesce. At occasional meetings for parents, one of the mothers with emerging consciousness on matters of gender (or, almost as likely, one of the fathers with emerging consciousness on matters of gender) might ask if anything could be done about the boys monopolizing the block corner; based on my exposure to the parents of that school, I wrote a story about a feminist father who gives his little girl a catcher's mitt for Christmas only to have her plant a marigold in it. The main event of the parents' meeting, though, was always a presentation from some member of the staff, who would lecture us about the habits and predilections of "the four-year-old." I knew that the staff was simply trying to prepare us for behavior that might otherwise throw inexperienced parents off balance, but I eventually announced to Alice that I thought we'd have to give up either the meetings or the school.

"I don't want to hear anyone tell me about 'the four-year-old,'" I said. "I live with one."

Also, I didn't like thinking of Abigail as "the four-year-old." It made her sound like a category instead of Abigail. Nothing up to that time had led me to believe that she was going to behave according to some established formula. Shortly after Abigail's third birthday, for instance, someone said to us, "I guess you're relieved to be done with those Terrible Twos." Alice and I exchanged looks. We'd realized that somehow we had totally forgotten about the Terrible Twos. No wonder: looking back over the previous twelve months, I couldn't think of anything terrible about them at all. In fact, two years old seems to me a particularly charming age for a little girl to be, at least the little girls who have been around our house. When we were being told about what to expect from "the four-year-old," our younger daughter, Sarah, had recently celebrated her first birthday, and I didn't think of her as "the one-year-old." She was already extremely Sarah-like, even though it was a few years before she was able to articulate her Sarahness precisely by announcing periodically that she was from the Planet Green, where people like her were considered regular and people like Abigail and Alice and me were thought of as a little bit weird. ("A classic expression of the second child's world-view," the staff person at the parents' meeting might have said if I had revealed such a remark instead of sitting there in sullen silence.)

I've always thought that handing out child-rearing advice is futile anyway, because parents — even parents who have eagerly solicited the advice — are not terribly likely to follow it. Nothing would be gained, for instance, by telling new parents that in early trips to the zoo it pays to follow Mies van der Rohe's dictum about less being more. When the child is so tired that he barely has enough energy to jam his cotton candy into his mother's hairdo, his father is still going to say, "But we can't leave without showing him the elephants!" Also, for most people, the process of rearing children is so all-encompassing that there isn't any way to adhere to any policy that doesn't coincide with their natural way of doing things. Getting advice on the best way to bring up children is like getting advice on the best way to breathe; sooner or later, you're probably going to forget it and go back to your regular old in-and-out. Most children spend enough time with their parents to see through the veneer of an officially adopted policy and focus on the lessons they're being taught by watching the grown-ups behave. Although I rather doubt that many parents are able to alter their normal behavior in the long run by remembering that they're setting an example for their children, there are obviously examples of short-term alterations — the time, for instance, when I found a twenty-dollar bill on Hudson Street.

Quite late one evening, when the girls were still small, Alice and I were walking toward our house, in Greenwich Village, when I spotted a twenty-dollar bill on the sidewalk. As I picked it up, Alice said, "You'll have to turn it in." I must have given her a puzzled look, because she added, "Some poor person could have dropped it." The next morning, she reminded me that I was going to go over to the Sixth Precinct to turn in the twenty.

"It's not that I believe in keeping property that is not my own," I said. "As you know, I was strictly raised about such matters. Of course, that was in Kansas City, in a different era. In New York these days, I think it's fair to say, there's a certain amount of cynicism abroad — big city, different times, and all that. What I'm afraid of, frankly, is that I'll walk into the Sixth

Precinct, announce that I want to turn in twenty dollars in cash that I found on Hudson Street late at night, and get myself hauled off to Bellevue as a loony. I've heard they can keep you there twenty-four hours for observation, no matter what."

"I've already told the girls that you're going over there to turn it in," Alice said. She could have just as easily said, "I've been officially informed by a representative of the Lord that if you don't turn in the twenty-dollar bill a bolt of lightning will fry you to a crisp."

"I'm off," I said, reaching for my coat.

The sergeant at the Sixth Precinct did not have me hauled off to Bellevue. He just said something like "Let me get this straight: you found this twenty-dollar bill last night and you want to turn it in for somebody to claim?"

"That's right, Sergeant," I said. I had decided not to trouble him with the part about the poor person.

He exchanged glances with a patrolman who was sitting nearby. Then he reached for a form, and began to fill it out. A sergeant who worked in the Sixth Precinct, which is responsible for the Village, was obviously someone who'd been exposed to a broad range of human behavior. For all I knew, there could be a man on Perry Street who regularly turned in his own fifties, just as a sort of hobby. A few months later, to my amazement, I got a notice from police headquarters downtown that, the twenty having gone unclaimed, I could come down and pick it up. I did. I told the girls.

I should also say that I'm still not completely convinced that, given the variety of children and parents and circumstances and chance, one technique of child rearing is necessarily preferable to another. I once came across a study that a social scientist had done comparing child-rearing policies among residents of

New York's Chinatown to the child-rearing policies of white middle-class people in the Massachusetts college town where he lived and taught. It immediately occurred to me, of course, that he might be someone who enjoyed life in a comfortable college town except for the Chinese-food deprivation that sometimes afflicts academics who find themselves too far from someplace like New York or San Francisco or Los Angeles. If I had been in his shoes, one of my first priorities would have been to figure out how to arrange some binge trips to Chinatown restaurants, and he had obviously made the arrangements in a way that permitted him to get along with his work at the same time. In other words, even before I read the study, I was prepared to treat it as the work of a pretty savvy researcher.

As I recall the results of the study, what it found was that, compared with the white middle-class Massachusetts people, Chinatown parents were, on the whole, remarkably permissive. They didn't get terribly excited when the room was untidy or the chores were neglected or the kid was up way past his bed-time — if, in fact, he had a bedtime. But there was one area in which they were much stricter than the Massachusetts parents. When it came to fighting with or tormenting or belittling a sibling, the Chinatown parents were murder. They simply wouldn't stand for it. Could it be, I asked myself when I read this, that the social scientist had come across an essential secret of child rearing? Then another thought occurred to me: why was I assuming that the Chinatown kids turned out so much better than the Massachusetts kids simply because their food was so much better?

What seemed to make sense within the context of the way Chinese-American families are organized might not make as much sense for a Yankee academic family in Massachusetts, of course, but the cultural gap doesn't have to be wide for there to be a wide difference in attitude. When some people I know—people of background and education similar to ours—took their first family trip to Europe, they required their children to write reports every evening on the sights they had seen that day, a policy that I would have thought could trigger a visit from a social worker prepared to deliver a stern lecture on the variety of forms child abuse can take. Some other people I know spent years of being joined in bed virtually every night by one or another of their children who felt the need of companionship, behavior that I think would have eventually provoked me into calling the police. I like both sets of these parents. I like their children, all of whom managed to grow up without doing any jail time. Sometimes, I find myself drawn to the simplest possible way of explaining what may count in rearing children: your children are either the center of your life or they're not, and the rest is commentary.

I don't mean that I've never heard any child-rearing tips that made sense, only that they made sense partly because they coincided with the way we were likely to go about things anyway. When Abigail was still a baby, a friend of ours from Kansas City—a businessman whose three children were already grown—told me that one of the happiest decisions he'd made when his kids were small was to become the official breakfast giver of the household. He had liked the idea of his wife getting a few more minutes of snoozing before one of the kids went up to ask her if she'd seen the purple mittens; he had liked having the kids to himself for a while in the morning. As it happened, we had already moved in that direction. Because I happen to wake up earlier than Alice does, I was doing the early-morning bottle. The bottle evolved into breakfast, and that lasted through high school.

I loved giving breakfast to the girls. I loved it when giving them breakfast meant a bottle or baby food, and I loved it after Abigail became old enough to understand that, remarkable as I was, I did not deserve total credit for making such good cornflakes. (Sarah knew from just about the start that I didn't deserve credit for the cornflakes; her older sister, in an early display of generational loyalty, ratted me out on that one.) Sometimes, I used our breakfast gathering to talk about my own childhood in Kansas City — the terroristic attacks by chiggers, the complete absence of bubble gum during World War II, the disorienting feeling of living in a world without zip codes. In other words, I tried to fulfill the mandate every American has to convince his children that they have a cushy deal compared with the deprivations and tribulations he had to face as a child. At one point, of course, I had to quit telling them that when I was a little boy in Kansas City my sister, Sukey, and I walked ten miles barefoot through the snow just to get to school every morning. They got old enough to check it out.

That is always an awkward transition for a parent — the onset of what I think of as the age of independent confirmation of data. It seems to come rather suddenly. One moment, your daughters are accepting everything you say without reservation, asking again for the story about how, when you met Mommy, you thought it would be romantic to take her to the Bronx Zoo to see the takin, which is the single smelliest animal in the world. The next moment, you've got a couple of private eyes in the house. They want to know precisely how smelliness in animals is measured. On trips to Kansas City that are supposed to be relaxed family visits, they're counting off blocks between school and the old homestead, grilling the grandmother incessantly, gathering information from an aunt who is somehow under the impression that she and her brother had to walk only eight blocks to school and were adequately shod and were transported in the car by their mother at the slightest hint of inclement weather.

"I suppose Aunt Sukey denies that during the war we were without bubble gum for months on end," I'd say, when the girls, apparently overinfluenced by Nancy Drew, had returned from a fact-finding mission to Kansas City.

"She says that your daddy could get bubble gum because he was a grocer," they'd say. "But she says that you couldn't seem to figure out how to blow bubbles anyway."

"Poor Sukey," I'd say. "Her memory's going."

Even after the onset of independent confirmation of data, I continued to give the girls breakfast. I was not even put off when they suddenly boycotted my scrambled eggs. One morning, obviously having conspired together in advance, they announced, courteously, that they would no longer eat my scrambled eggs. The word "yucky" was used. So was the word "disgusting"—although, as someone with serious responsibilities in the area of the girls' grammar and syntax, I reminded them that the phrase "yucky and disgusting" is mildly redundant. Naturally, I objected to their decision. "What is this, a selective hunger strike?" I said. "Have we somehow raised a couple of Bolsheviks here?" They wouldn't budge. After some consideration, I realized that I couldn't blame them. Years later, I was asked to contribute a recipe to a charity cookbook, and the only recipe I had was for the scrambled eggs I'd given the girls every morning; I called them "Scrambled Eggs That Stick to the Pan Every Time." The more I thought of what those eggs were like, the more I had to admire the girls for taking matters into their own hands.

I was, somehow, astonished when our breakfasts together ended. When Sarah began applying to colleges, I admitted in a column that somewhere in my mind I must have always taken it for granted that she'd be going to New York University, which is in the neighborhood, so I wouldn't need a sleepover when I came by at breakfast to cut the crusts off her toast. As far as I could tell, the time that had elapsed between Abigail getting an early-morning bottle and both of them having breakfast in a college dining hall was about fifteen minutes. I began to regret all those times when having to report a story out of town had kept me from presiding over breakfast. By saying that, I don't mean to suggest to new fathers that they somehow arrange their schedules in a way that permits them to be the household breakfast giver every morning. They're on their own.

2

The Evil Eye, the Tiny Deflator

E ven if I were more inclined than I am to hand out advice that may be inappropriate and would probably be ignored anyway, I would be constrained by another consideration: the Evil Eye. People who treat the Evil Eye with some respect can tell you that anyone dispensing advice about family—and thus implying that he and his own family are so blessed, so close to perfection that it behooves them to share with others the secret of their success—is asking for trouble. I am talking now simply about people who treat the Evil Eye with some respect; true believers in the Evil Eye might even look upon a statement that your children haven't done any jail time as a way to invite a late-night call from a bail bondsman.

The Evil Eye is not spoken of much in modern American life. Among the young, you don't often even hear someone hedge his bet with a simple "knock on wood." The sort of public officials who are always lecturing us about family values seem not to fear the Evil Eye, any more than they seem to fear the possibility that some reporter might find it entertaining to un- cover the circumstances of their last divorce or point out that they missed both of their children's high school graduation cer- emonies. I'm not superstitious myself. I don't avoid black cats any more than I avoid cats of any color. Alice and I were married on Friday the 13th. I have never acknowledged that there is any su- perstition behind my policy of not resetting my watch until an airplane I'm flying in actually lands in the new time zone. To me, remaining on the old time until we're back on the ground is simply a technique for keeping the plane in the air — a technique that has so far proven effective. Do I personally believe in the Evil Eye? Not exactly. All right, maybe a little bit.

Once, at the annual antiquarian book fair of PS 3, the slightly cockamamie and ultimately splendid Greenwich Vil- lage grade school that both of our girls attended after the words- not-hands nursery school, I happened upon a thick, serious- looking English-Yiddish dictionary. Even though Spanish and Russian and Cantonese have become more common than Yid- dish in New York subways, Yiddish remains for New Yorkers the language of contention. I've always thought that visitors to the city should be given Yiddish phrase books by the New York Convention and Visitors Bureau, except that instead of having phrases like "Could you please direct me to the nearest post office?" the New York phrase book would have phrases like "May boils break out on your liver!" or "May streetcars grow in the back of your throat!" At the time I spotted this dictionary, I owned two English-Yiddish dictionaries — Leo Rosten's *Joys of Yiddish* and a volume called *Dictionary Shmictionary* — but both of them are antic and anecdotal. I had never seen a serious English-Yiddish dictionary. I started leafing through it, and came to the word *mees*, which means ugly. (An ugly person is a *meeskeit*, rhyming with "geese bite"; there's a song by that name in *Cabaret*.) The first definition offered was, not surprisingly, "ugly." The second definition was "beautiful." That definition was followed by the explanation, in parentheses: "so as to fool the Evil Eye."

I found myself with two immediate responses. One was "What a language!" It's no wonder that in New York Irish cops and Bangladeshi cabdrivers and Dominican grocers feel the need to employ it in stressful moments. It's no wonder so many people are horrified at the prospect of its dying out. In what other language could one word mean both ugly and beautiful? My other response was that the custom alluded to by the second definition—calling someone who's beautiful, particularly a beautiful child, a *meeskeit* just in case the Evil Eye happens to be tuned in might not be such a bad idea. As the advertisements for the New York State Lottery say, "Hey, you never know."

So have I never said anything about my children that might tempt the Evil Eye? It has to be said that there is a certain amount of tension between respect for the power of the Evil Eye and a parent's natural inclination to brag about his children. I happen to come from a tradition of bragging about children. My father—a mild-mannered man who wouldn't have struck anyone as a boaster or a show-off—used to travel a lot after he was more or less retired, and he often said to other travelers he met, "I'll show you a picture of my grandchildren if you promise that you won't go home and throw rocks at your own grandchildren." I've always been suspicious of parents who don't brag about their children. (When it comes to parents who routinely put down their children in conversations with casual acquaintances, I'm more than just suspicious. I think they should be arrested; if no charges stick, at least they'd have a chance of being roughed up at the station house.) If I run into someone who has a small child and is not carrying pictures, I start to wonder. "Has the kid turned mean and ugly, or what?" I ask. When someone I know becomes the father of a girl, I send him a sign that a kind man I knew in Tampa printed for me on a press he kept in his garage. On a light blue background is a quotation we've credited to President Franklin Pierce (he had so few): "Anyone who is not objectionable about his daughter is a pervert." Some of the new fathers put the sign on their office wall. Some of them use it as the center of a montage whose other elements are pictures of their daughter. Either way, it functions as an easement for excessive bragging.

I've tried to show some restraint, particularly in print. (The Evil Eye is known to be a voracious reader.) I haven't always managed. When Abigail was about six months old, Alice and I went to a dinner party on the West Side and were drawn into a conversation with other parents about whether it was safe for people who lived in Manhattan to leave a baby in a carriage on the sidewalk for just a few seconds while ducking into a store for, say, a newspaper. Many years later, there was a brief flutter of publicity in New York about two or three incidents of European visitors leaving their children unattended—in one case, in a baby carriage outside a bar—while they went about their business, only to have concerned New Yorkers call 911. Commentators took the occasion to point out that Europeans did not have the intense interest Americans do in the protection and entertainment of children—meaning that, depending on the way you look at it, either Europe is a more mature culture or Europeans miss out on a lot of fun. One of the European parents involved said that leaving your baby in a carriage outside a saloon was common practice in Copenhagen, Denmark, a position that was answered in one of the tabloids under the headline "From the Folks Who Brought You Flimsy Furniture."

When the subject came up at the dinner party, I did not claim any cultural differences between the Village and the West Side. I said that it seemed to me to depend on the quality of the baby. "It would probably be O.K. if you had an ordinary baby," I heard myself saying. The other parents stared at me. It dawned on me that not many of them thought they had ordinary babies. Having already begun, though, I had to explain that a peek at my daughter in a baby carriage could trigger latent kidnapping instincts in the most saintly passerby. If I had already come across the English-Yiddish dictionary, I suppose I would have ended my explanation by winking at them conspiratorially and saying, "You see, she's a real *meeskeit*." If the contretemps involving the baby left outside of the bar had already taken place, I suppose I might have added, "The point is not that the mother couldn't have been much of a mother but that the baby couldn't have been much of a baby."

The perils inherent in being self-satisfied about your family are not limited to the Evil Eye. The Tiny Deflator is also a threat—that small voice from the backseat that makes you realize that what you just said was, upon reflection, pretentious or silly or, if we're being absolutely literal about it, not strictly true. Almost all children can take the role of the Tiny Deflator, although some play it better than others. It may help to be from the Planet Green. When our daughters were on the edge of being old enough to take to the ballet, we decided they might like a Sunday matinee program at Lincoln Center that included

Parade—a jolly piece, famous for its backdrops by Picasso. As it turned out, we were right. The girls were entranced. Nobody got restless or cranky, not even me. After the performance, Alice thought of going to the Seagram Building, so that we could show Abigail and Sarah the Picasso backdrop in the Four Seasons restaurant. We all loved that, too. After the viewing, we went downstairs to the Brasserie, the restaurant on the ground floor, and had tea—which is to say, if it was a typical tea in our family in that era, Alice had tea, the girls had ice cream and I had a scotch. The girls, I have to say, were looking particularly fetching in their special-event clothes. It was a period when they looked so fetching in their special-event clothes that some neighbors we hardly knew who were holding a wedding in the courtyard next to our house asked if our daughters could come to the ceremony in some rather Victorian dresses the girls then had—acting as what people in New Orleans sometimes call scene-boosters. Just as our tea was ending, Sarah suddenly said, "You know, our family is different from other families."

Alice beamed. I may have beamed myself. I'm not much of a beamer, but it was, I thought, a special moment. I suppose Alice and I had been thinking thoughts not that far removed from what Sarah had expressed. We were feeling fortunate.

"Some families put a lot of toothpaste on their toothbrushes," Sarah continued. "But in our family, we don't put very much." The beams must have faded involuntarily, and Sarah must have noticed. "Also," she began, trying to save the moment, "our family has a special tuna fish recipe."

Twenty years or so after that outing, our entire family was in a hospital room, listening to the regimen the doctor expected me to follow when I went home to continue recuperating from heart bypass surgery—how often I was to nap, how I was to avoid long periods at my desk. We all nodded soberly. When he had finished, I tried to look both brave and prudent. Then Abigail said, "I hate to say it, Daddy, but it's hard to see just how that differs from your regular routine." A Tiny Deflator, all grown up.

3

Be Careful What You Say in Front of Daddy

There were, of course, only the four of us in that booth at the Brasserie when the Tiny Deflator struck with the toothpaste formula she'd been saving for the occasion, but members of a writer's family, even as children, live in peril of being overheard by the general public. I've always thought it only fair to remind Alice of that regularly. We might be having a quiet dinner together at the end of a busy day—just the two of us, now that the girls are out of the house—and Alice might have just shared some observation of the sort that married couples feel comfortable in exchanging. Even after all these years, she sometimes seems a bit startled when I say, in response, "I hope you're not under the impression that what you just said was off the record, Alice. Nobody mentioned anything about deep background or not for attribution or anything like that."

Some writers are not even satisfied to lie in wait for quotable remarks. Their families face the dangers of what amounts to entrapment. Many years ago, I worked with someone whose novels of young married life were thought to be more fact than fiction. When he wasn't in evidence at the office late in the afternoon, one of his colleagues would say something like "He mentioned that he was having trouble with the chapter on the breakup, so I figure he went home early to try to goad Betsy into an argument." You might suggest that people who, through no fault of their own, live in the same house as a writer should simply make it their business to utter no quotable remarks—communicating in common phrases that are certain not to stir the writer's interest, nodding or shaking the head whenever that will do, prefacing any potentially embarrassing statement with some phrase like "I would like to say something now that is completely off the record" or "I've called you together for a background session on the broken lamp, and I want to start by getting the ground rules straight on what can and can't be quoted." Even that, though, would not actually give them complete protection against exposure. Anything they did, even silently, could find its way into print. This vulnerability does not even have a statute of limitations.

There is often a connection between the way someone writes about his own family and the way he's written about the family he came from. It's common these days for memoirs of childhood to concentrate on some dark secret within the author's ostensibly happy family. I've admired some of those memoirs, but I've always known that I wouldn't be writing one of them. The material just wasn't there. At times, in fact, I've imagined myself at some bar late at night with writers who have dealt with such issues. After discussing their own upbringings for a while, they look toward me. Their looks are not totally respectful. They are aware that I've admitted in print that I never heard my parents raise their voices to each other. They have reason to suspect, from bits of information I've let drop from time to time, that I was happy in high school. I try desperately to think of a dark secret in my upbringing. All I can think of is Chubby, the collie dog.

"Well, there's Chubby, the collie dog," I say tentatively.

"Chubby, the collie dog?" they repeat.

There really was a collie named Chubby. I wouldn't claim that the secret about him qualifies as certifiably traumatic, but maybe it explains an otherwise mysterious loyalty I had as a boy to the collie stories of Albert Payson Terhune. We owned Chubby when I was two or three years old. Apparently, he was sickly. One day my parents told Sukey and me that he had been given to some friends who lived on a farm, so that he could thrive in the healthy country air. Many years later—as I remember, I was home on vacation from college—Chubby's name came up while my parents and Sukey and I were having dinner. I asked why we'd never gone to visit him on the farm. I had a faint memory from childhood of my parents saying that we were no longer friends with the people who owned the farm. Sukey looked at me as if I had suddenly announced that I was thinking about eating the mashed potatoes with my hands for a while, just for a change of pace.

"There wasn't any farm," she said. "That was just what they told us. Chubby had to be put to sleep. You never knew that?"

"Put to sleep!" I said. "Chubby's gone?"

Somebody—my mother, I think—pointed out that Chubby would have been gone in any case, since collies didn't ordinarily live to the age of eighteen.

"Isn't it sort of late for me to be finding this out?" I said.

"It's not our fault if you're slow on the uptake," my father said.

I once decided to dedicate a book to Sukey, and my first draft of the dedication was "To my sister, Sukey Fox, as a first tentative step toward forgiving her for attempting to push me down the laundry chute in 1937."

Alice strongly advised that I take out the reference to the laundry chute incident, and not simply because quite a few decades had passed since the alleged attack—so many, in fact, that there might be any number of readers who'd be puzzled by the reference because they wouldn't know what a laundry chute was. Mentioning the laundry chute, Alice said, was "not terribly gracious."

"Neither is attempted murder," I said.

But I did take out the reference to the laundry chute. Not that Sukey would have minded having it mentioned; I've heard her boast about the deed. She likes to talk about how I was saved by being too fat to fit through the chute. If she had said something while she did her best to cram me through the little door—"Heh, heh, heh," maybe, or "This'll teach you to be so adorable" or "I'm simply acting out a perfectly normal response of a first child who sees her place in the family usurped"—I'm sure she would have been happy to have that reported, too.

But what if Sukey had actually been embarrassed at having been caught in an attempt to annihilate her baby brother? Or what if she, as a child or as an adult, had done something else she'd just as soon not have me share with the population at large? What if, for instance, she had a serious drinking problem that she'd rather not see widely discussed? (I think that in Sukey's case problem drinking is safe to use as an example without raising suspicions among her friends and neighbors that it might actually be true: I once described her in print—quite accurately, she later confirmed—as "someone whose intake of strong drink has always been limited to a chocolate-marshmallow daiquiri every other New Year's Eve.") There are writers, I realize, who would say that a writer's obligation to his art should transcend any qualms he might have about revealing something that would wound or humiliate someone in his family. I would argue that it depends on the quality of the art, just as the question of whether or not to leave a baby unattended for a moment or two depends on the quality of the baby.

When this subject happens to come up, I have a simple rule of thumb that I offer to my fellow scribblers. I call it the Dostoyevsky test: If you have reason to believe that you're another Dostoyevsky, there is no reason to be concerned about the effect what you write might have on the life of some member of your family. Your art is considerably more important than any such consideration. Readers a century or two from now should not be deprived of the prose you fashion out of, say, the circumstances leading to your conclusion that your oldest son simply didn't have the guts to stick to junior-varsity football and thus set a pattern for a life of drifting. You have the right—the responsibility, really, to future generations of readers—to mention your mother's private confession to you, in a moment of stress, that she never truly loved your father, even if putting that confession in print causes some awkwardness in their life at the retirement village. If you have reason to believe that you're another Dostoyevsky, you can say anything you need to say. If you don't have reason to believe that you're another Dostoyevsky, you can't.

Thinking about how writers deal with the question of using their families as material, it has occurred to me that I may be—

of all the things that nobody wants to be—a moderate. On one end of the spectrum are writers who seem to yearn mostly for a high score on the reveal-o-meter—people who can work in, say, a husband's sexual dysfunction or at least a daughter's humiliation at the hands of a prom date into an article whose ostensible subject is the changing American views of cranberry sauce and turkey stuffing as holiday side dishes. At the other end are writers who believe that any mention of your family in print is exploitation on the order of a lounge comic doing cheap jokes about his wife. The differences obviously can be accounted for partly by cultural and generational differences. Around our house, we sometimes refer to people who are uncomfortable with writing about their private lives as "fifties guys." People at the other end of the spectrum are likely to have grown up at a later time or to have been raised in those small patches of the East Coast and the West Coast where anyone who does not come right out and say that he deeply resents his father for sleeping with his mother is assumed to be dissembling.

When it comes to the tone of voice used in writing about family there is also a spectrum, ranging roughly from sitcom to movie of the week. It may be that someone who can't do any better at childhood trauma than the laundry chute incident or the disappearance of Chubby was programmed early on to operate toward the sitcom end. The writing I've done on grim subjects—murders, for instance—has almost always concerned strangers, and it has almost always been written without use of the first person singular. Alice and the girls began appearing only in lighter pieces—pieces about travel or eating or the little domestic dramas that in the American tradition (and certainly in the tradition of our family) tend to be about the manipulation of the father. In the first book I did about eating, *American Fried*, Alice's role in the sitcom was established as that of the levelheaded wife who had some sense of restraint herself (except, perhaps, when it came to ice cream) and spent a lot of time trying to rein in the cheerful glutton she found herself married to. She was, if I may be permitted an inappropriate phrase, the straight man. Once, Alice and I both spoke to a conference of English teachers in Indiana. She was then involved in trying to find ways of teaching basic writing to underprepared students, having become, as I often explained to people, a college English teacher who'd worked her way down from Shakespeare to the simple sentence. Joe Trimmer, of Ball State University, the professor who had invited us to speak, introduced us to the audience by saying, "They're like Burns and Allen, except she's George and he's Gracie."

In the books I wrote about eating, the girls were present at first mainly as children who ate the way most children eat. "While I'm speaking in Alice's defense, I should also say that I consider her failure with the children half my own," I wrote in one of the books. "No one person could be responsible for engendering in two innocent little girls a preference for frozen fish sticks over fish. In fact, in Nova Scotia, where we live in the summer, I have seen Alice take a flounder that was on a fishing boat an hour before, sprinkle it ever so slightly with some home-ground flour, fry it for a few seconds, and present it to her very own little girls—only to have them pick at it for a few minutes and gaze longingly toward the freezer."

Of course, the roles played in the sitcom paralleled real life. Like the Alice persona, the real Alice has tried to exercise some restraint (except, perhaps, when it came to ice cream) on the way we eat. For a while, the girls really did seem to prefer fish sticks to fish. At around the age of four, Sarah really did refuse to return to an afternoon play program she'd been attending in Kansas City while visiting her grandmother because they had the effrontery to serve her salad. "To this day she says, 'They gave me salad!' " I wrote a couple of years after that episode, "in the tone a countess roughly handled by the customs man might say, 'They searched my gown!' "

Once it has been established, a family sitcom may not turn into a movie of the week even if something terribly serious happens to the family being portrayed. In the seventies, when the girls were four and seven, something terribly serious happened to us: Alice was operated on for lung cancer. The summer after her operation, I was finishing the second of what turned out to be three books about eating—a series we eventually came to refer to around the house as the tummy trilogy. The work I did on the final drafts of the book was dominated by additional references to Alice. The first chapter began: "Now that it's fashionable to reveal intimate details of married life, I can state publicly that my wife, Alice, has a weird predilection for limiting our family to three meals a day." That chapter was called "Alice" and the last chapter was called "Alice's Treat." The title I eventually settled on for the book was *Alice, Let's Eat*.

At the time I thought that increasing Alice's role was a way to help knit together a book whose chapters ranged from a search for barbecued mutton in Kentucky (where I finally did find a restaurant with a sign that said "Mary Had a Little Lamb—Won't You Have Some Too") to a report on our friend Fats Goldberg at the opening of a Smithsonian Institution Bicentennial exhibition that included among its neon signs the logo of his own establishment, Goldberg's Pizzeria. Aside from trying to focus the book, though, I suppose I was conscious that spreading Alice from beginning to end in her usual George Burns role was a way of declaring, mainly to myself, that we were not accepting the prognosis that would have made her a tragic character. Also, tragic characters did not happen to be my specialty. If Alice had been married to a different sort of writer, she might have been presented in the sort of role Ali MacGraw played in *Love Story*, instead of in a role she has sometimes described as "a dietician in sensible shoes." It does seem unfair, I told Alice years later, but we all have to construct our little stories with the tools available to us.

A dozen years later, on Alice's fiftieth birthday, I wrote a poem to her whose first stanza was:

"No way," you say.
"It simply cannot be.
I would have guessed
That barmen often ask her for ID."
"I know, I know.
She has that youthful glow
That still gives young men vapors.
She's fifty, though. I've seen her papers."

I've recited that stanza in public any number of times. On the other hand, I wouldn't think of reciting some of the other stanzas, because they involve matters that are for me, a fifties guy at heart, private. For me — and, I suspect, for a number of other moderates — the line between what is on and off limits in writing about family has appeared naturally. Looking back at the years in question, for instance, I realize that, except for a few innocuous mentions, I didn't discuss my daughters in articles or books during the time that they could be roughly classified as teenagers. I suppose I took it for granted that those years were not an absolutely perfect time to have your father making wry remarks about you in print. Not that the girls suddenly turned into different creatures when they became teenagers. The conversation I had with Abigail when she came down to breakfast on her thirteenth birthday happily turned out to be a harbinger of the years to come. "Well, you're a teenager now," I said. "You want to throw a snit or something while I get the cereal?"

"I don't think so," she said. "I'm tired and I'm running a little late this morning."

I don't want to leave the impression that in those years we never witnessed one argument about who could borrow whose sweaters or that we never had to deal with a crisis of romance. It's just that I don't remember the teenage years as an entirely separate era, the way I remember World War II. I once read about a study indicating that a significant percentage of young people in America go from being thirteen to nineteen without exhibiting a lot of the behavior we've come to associate with teenagers. I'm sure that's true—although my first response was to wonder how the researchers went about gathering their data. A couple of the questions must have been "How many times today have you, in a weary and slightly disgusted voice, said, 'Oh, Mother'?" and "What is your record for number of questions answered at the dinner table with a grunt?" The questioning of teenage boys must have included a variety of ways of measuring long silences in the presence of parents seeking information. I once wrote about a couple I called Hank and Betsy Garland and their son Nick, a college student who, in the view of his parents, must have seen too many movies about how prisoners of war are supposed to say nothing beyond their name, rank and serial number. At the dinner table, Betsy Garland might say something to Nick like "So apparently the Miller boy has decided to go to law school because he figures a law degree will never hurt you, whether you actually practice or not, and he thinks it's the sort of thing you're better off doing right away because if not, who knows when you'll ever feel like going back to school even if you think it's basically something that will stand you in good stead, which makes a lot of sense to me, doesn't it to you, Nick?"

And Nick would say, if he was in a particularly loquacious mood, "I guess."

When Sarah was about twelve, she figured in a piece I did in Paris about checking the authenticity of French attempts at American fast-food hamburgers; she and a couple of kids we knew who lived in Paris accompanied me to places like the Burger King on the Champs-Elysées ("Maison du Whopper") and to at least one place so far from authenticity that its hamburgers were rectangular. The last article that I think of as having Sarah in the starring role, though, concerned a trip she and I took when she was ten to the Fourth Annual St. Johns River Catfish Festival in Crescent City, Florida, ostensibly for the purpose of determining whether or not she would try catfish. I say "ostensibly," because anyone who had been reading about Sarah in those days would have taken the bald statement of our mission as the equivalent of saying that you're taking a strict Muslim cleric from Saudi Arabia to Tennessee to see if he might like to participate in a typical American hog roast.

Sarah had emerged as the Picky Eater in our repertory troupe. She played the role beautifully. By then, she had coined a phrase for supposedly edible substances that she found revolting: "guts and throwup." (We still use the phrase in our family, and it has never been criticized for not being sufficiently evocative.) She was totally unapologetic about her tastes. For a while, we were in the habit of stopping on the way to Nova Scotia at a legendary Maine lobster shack, where we would order three lobsters plus a tuna fish sandwich for Sarah. At some point during the meal, she could be counted on to say something like "The tuna fish here is excellent. Yes, excellent!" I've never had a more enjoyable trip than the one Sarah and I took to Florida, but Sarah ate no catfish. She also did not eat frog legs, cooter, gator tail or swamp cabbage. When readers got what turned out to be the last clear close-up they were going to get of Sarah for several years, she is standing in a park in Crescent City, Florida, where a lot of other people are lined up for a catfish dinner. She is shaking her head. I am assuring her that catfish tastes like flounder. She is saying, "Does it taste like chocolate?"

There were some mentions after that of a teenager who had some characteristics in common with Sarah. When she was about sixteen—well within the privacy DMZ—I found myself wanting to write a couple of newspaper columns that were based roughly on her experiences. One of them was about the elaborate plan concocted by a sixteen-year-old girl to get the perfect tan during spring vacation despite the efforts of the Sun Police, a squad of unimaginative flatfoots whose only weapon was nagging ("Will you please get out of the sun this minute!"). The other was about how anxiety over the approach of the Scholastic Aptitude Test's vocabulary section can inspire teenagers to employ the sort of words you wouldn't expect to hear from them. In both cases, I asked Sarah how she'd feel about my writing about someone named S. She would, of course, be given the opportunity to go over the manuscript, like a wartime censor in charge of excising any sensitive material. She agreed. So I did a column on the tan plan and a column on pre-SAT vocabulary. The latter began with what I believe was an exact quotation of what I'd said to Sarah at breakfast one morning:

" 'Relax,' I kept saying to S., the teenager I know best, as the pressure in her crowd mounted. 'I read that a lot of colleges don't pay much attention to SAT scores anyway. Also, you can always go to work in the dime store.'

" 'Relaxing would be a herculean task—meaning a task very difficult to perform,' S. said. 'Because among my friends there's no dearth of anxieties. A dearth is like a paucity—a scarcity or scanty supply. In fact, most of the people I know have a plethora of anxieties—a surfeit, an overabundance.' "

In those window-of-privacy years, I also wrote some columns about a father and a daughter talking at breakfast—the conversations were always carried on in conjunction with a discussion of the riboflavin content of various cereals—but the daughter I wrote about was generic. (In fact, long after Abigail and Sarah left home, the generic daughter was still available to be written about—a poor substitute for the real thing.) I suppose the girls began returning to print as themselves when I wrote about Abigail during her junior year in college. She had decided to spend a semester in Madrid as a way of becoming fluent in Spanish— a decision that delighted me, although, as someone who had thrown himself against the Spanish language regularly without success for thirty years, I asked her during her first phone call from Spain if she knew the Spanish word for "envious." After a trip to visit Abigail in Madrid, I wrote a piece called "Abigail y Yo," in which I acknowledged that when I think of my obituary—people who have spent much of their lives as reporters are often afflicted with the ability to imagine their own obituary, a decent-sized death notice having traditionally been the principal side benefit of the trade—the drop head I have sometimes imagined is "Monolingual Reporter Succumbs."

As it turned out, I hadn't stopped writing about Sarah soon enough. When she was about six, I mentioned in print that when we went to dinner in Chinatown she always carried along a bagel, just in case. I even wrote, I regret to say, that there were times when, preparing to leave the house for Chinatown without having remembered that requirement, we heard a small voice say, "My bagel! My bagel!" It somehow hadn't occurred to me that readers would tend to freeze the habits of her childhood in their mind, so that when Sarah was in college people she met were asking her if she still carried a bagel with her to Chinatown. As it happened, Sarah loved Chinese food by then and was not pleased by the assumption that she required a security bagel while dining in a Chinese restaurant. I have, of course, informed Sarah that, in the spirit of those people we sometimes read about who have spent decades trying to overturn the unjust court-martial of a Civil War ancestor, I intend to devote my sunset years to correcting the notion that she continues to carry a bagel to Chinatown. I often mention it when speaking in public. She declined my offer to have her videotaped arriving at the corner of Mott and Bayard, being searched for bagels by an extremely professional homicide detective I'm acquainted with, and being declared clean. She thought that was more than the situation called for.

After my daughters were grown, I wrote a book about my father—partly, I think, to give Abigail and Sarah, who never got to meet him, some idea of what he was like. It was an affectionate book. I thought of it as a tribute, really, or maybe a thank-you. But the man portrayed was not meant as a persona. He was my father, complete with my father's foibles and my father's eccentricities. During the book tour, I called for questions one night after a reading in a bookstore, and someone asked if I was at all troubled by the possibility that one of my own daughters would someday write a book about me, as I had done about my father.

"Not at all," I answered. "And the reason I'm not worried is something I had them sign when they were about five and eight—a simple legal document. It's not elaborate, just the standard nondisclosure agreement—modeled on the one that, from what I understand, employees of Buckingham Palace are required to sign before being hired. Did they wonder about it? Well, yes. But I said, 'Just sign here, girls. Really. It's O.K. You know you can trust your daddy.' "

4

Cram Course

One Sunday morning, some years after the girls had made good on their implicit threat to grow up and lead lives of their own, Alice and I were lingering at the breakfast table, perusing the Sunday *New York Times* at our leisure. That sort of Sunday morning activity is common among people who aren't regularly being asked such questions as which section of the paper is available for lining the guinea pig cage. I happened to start with a story in the *Times* magazine about the Emanuel brothers, all of whom had become high achievers at an early age—Rahm Emanuel, an operative in the Clinton White House, and his equally high-powered brothers, one a prominent medical ethicist based at Harvard and one a rich Hollywood agent. The article said that while the brothers were growing up their parents quizzed them on current events at the dinner table every evening and scheduled a different cultural outing every Sunday.

Had we ever taken the girls to the ballet on Sunday except for that time we went to see *Parade*? I tried to focus my memory on Sunday with the girls. I could see us shopping for smoked salmon on the Lower East Side. I could see us in Chinatown. I could see us at Fats Goldberg's Pizzeria. I couldn't see any ballets. "Does *The Nutcracker* count?" I mumbled. Alice apparently didn't hear me.

I quit reading the article on the Emanuel brothers. Why should I be reminded that the plan I had devised to teach my daughters geography during the summer in Nova Scotia had never been put into effect? They can get whatever geographical information they need on the Internet anyway. It's been years since either one of them showed signs of thinking that Alabama is the capital of Chicago.

I turned to the main news section, where I read that during the childhoods of Robert and Ethel Kennedy's offspring, poetry was recited at dinner, current events were debated in the car, skiing was taught by an Olympic medal winner, and on summer mornings, laps in the ocean were followed by tennis lessons, sailing lessons, riding lessons and football, "all scheduled, as though it were camp."

"Hey! What's going on here?" I said. "Is it possible that, for some reason of their own, the editors of *The New York Times* are trying to make every parent in the New York metropolitan area feel shiftless?"

"Mmmmm," Alice said, from behind the Money & Business section.

The article in the *Times* reminded us that Robert and Ethel Kennedy had eleven children—many of whom, contrary to the common public perception, had never had any need for rehab facilities. I have nothing against the Kennedy offspring, but I decided I didn't want to finish the article about them. I was afraid I'd find that one of them had arranged for his own children to have chess lessons from Gary Kasparov at dawn every day, just before the rock-climbing instructor arrived.

Alice finished Money & Business and started to pass it to me, aware that I sometimes like to give it a quick once-over just in case some overpaid CEO has been caught in a particularly gruesome scandal. I said no, thanks. As I'd handed it to her across the breakfast table, I had noticed that the lead story was on a young Wall Street figure named Jonathan Steinberg, the son of the eighties corporate raider and conspicuous consumer Saul P. Steinberg. Given the rest of the news in the *Times* that morning, I wouldn't have been surprised if that story had included the information that Jonathan Steinberg and his siblings were, as children, made to earn an annualized 12 percent return on mock stock portfolios or lose their bathroom privileges.

Sports was out of the question. For weeks, the sports pages had been filled with tales of how Earl Woods had spent most of his waking hours training his son, Tiger, to be the greatest golfer in history — beginning, as I remember, with a 2-iron art fully redesigned so that it could be used by a baby not yet old enough to stand up. Given what I had seen of the paper so far, the Arts & Leisure section would probably have an article on a symphony conductor who'd been started on violin lessons at an age when my daughters were still being allowed to waste their time in blatantly unfocused play with their daddy.

I could imagine an inspector showing up from some outfit with a name like the Responsible Parenting League. He's carrying a checklist that he goes over in front of me, in the tone that might be used by a particularly severe customs inspector going over my declaration. "I see there is no SAT prep course listed," he says. "No language lessons. No tennis lessons. Perhaps you'd like to explain the set of blocks that is listed here under 'blatantly unfocused play with their daddy.' "

I could show him the blocks. We still have them. They're stored in a circular receptacle that's about twice the size of a snare drum and has casters on it, so it can be rolled out of storage space underneath the staircase. I still roll out the blocks whenever a child of a certain age comes to visit. The child's parents never seem to mind. Apparently, they're confident that the current events quizzes and riding lessons are all on schedule at home and that my house can therefore be treated as recess.

"The blocks came from a place called Creative Playthings," I say to the inspector. "It may be that you people give parents a few points just for dealing with a place that has a name like that."

The inspector is noncommittal. He is concentrating on the checklist, running his pencil down the page and making odd little clucking sounds. Could the Responsible Parenting League have an intelligence system good enough to know that the blocks came from Creative Playthings sort of by chance? I remember precisely how it happened. When Abigail was about three, she had a set of rather lifelike rubber figures—a mother and a father and a boy and a girl—whose limbs could be bent into a variety of shapes. While we were out of the city during the summer, both of the female figures got lost. I suppose I could have made a claim to the inspector that our eagerness to find replacements when we got back to New York was based on a concern that the absence of female figures could warp Abigail's perception in the entire area of gender identification, but I think the truth is that Abigail probably said more than once "I miss the mommy." At the store, we were informed that the rubber figures were being phased out, and were available only at the factory in Cranbury, New Jersey. Naturally, after placing Abigail in the care of the words-not-hands people one morning, we made our way to Cranbury, New Jersey. There we found sets of rubber people in great variety—not just family groups but groups of postmen and army officers and nurses. The sets had splendid names. As I remember, one of them was called "Bendable Integrated Rubber Work Group." There were also rubber animals, done in the same scale. At the factory in Cranbury, New Jersey, they were all on sale. So were the blocks.

With the blocks, we'd build houses and roads and bridges. Then we'd put in place a parade of rubber people, some of them riding rubber animals. Sometimes, for accompaniment, I'd put on one of the LPs of John Philip Sousa marches I'd inherited from my father, or a tape of a New Orleans brass band. The blocks had proven to be indestructible. Over time, most of the bendable rubber people lost their bendability— you'd push an African-American father's arm to his side and it would suddenly spring up, as if he were Richard Nixon throwing that jerky, awkward wave to a crowd—but we got years of use out of them before that happened. As a friend in Nova Scotia would have put it, those rubber people didn't owe us any money.

"Are you maintaining, then," the inspector continues, "that you were, through supervised block play, teaching the rudiments of how architects use space or laying the groundwork that would make it possible for the children to absorb, at a more appropriate age, the principles of engineering?"

"I'd rather not say," I reply. I keep thinking that the inspector reminds me of someone I'd written about before, and then I realize that he is very much like an immigration officer at Kennedy Airport I imagined meeting when we returned from the girls' first trip to France, when they were about eleven and fourteen. We had taken the girls to visit close friends in England fairly regularly, but for years I had said that children were ready to travel around the Continent about the time they were ready to eat a mushroom. I'd written about observing children on grand tours of Europe who were sitting in formal hotel dining rooms "doodling on the tablecloth with their butter knives, looking as if they were wondering whether there was any reason to hold out hope that they might be spared the second of tomorrow's scheduled cathedrals by a sudden downpour or perhaps a nuclear attack." But we'd decided that we might go even before the Mushroom Passage if, instead of dragging the poor things around on a grand tour, we plopped in a rented house in a French town—a method of world travel I called hanging around. That meant, of course, that we were going to be pretty short on certified sights when we arrived for what I envisioned as some trouble at Immigration:

" 'You must have loved the Tower of London, little lady,' the officer says to Sarah in a disarmingly friendly tone.

" 'We didn't actually go there,' Sarah says.

" 'Well,' he says, turning to Abigail with that same friendly air, 'the Colosseum in Rome must have been pretty exciting.'

" 'We were mainly just in this one town,' Abigail says. Then, sensing trouble, she adds, 'It was a very nice town.'

" 'The immigration officer turns to me, his voice coldly polite. 'I'm afraid I'll have to hold on to this passport of yours for a while, sir,' he says. 'Just routine.' "

As the inspector from the Responsible Parenting League resumes the task of ticking away at his checklist, a grim look on his face, I realize that we're getting poor marks once again. He is obviously too experienced to be taken in by those attempts some parents make to rationalize almost anything as an educational experience — to explain, for instance, that playing video games for six or eight hours a day is doing wonders for their son's hand-eye coordination. We obviously come up short in the sort of wide-bore pursuit of all-around self-improvement that the Kennedy kids were subjected to at Hickory Hill. We wouldn't be able to claim credit for any monomaniacal attempts to turn either of our daughters into a world champion in something like chess or platform diving.

Given the sort of intelligence network the inspector must have, he might even know that I was quietly relieved that neither of my daughters got caught up in one of the classic obsessions of little girls in America — horseback riding, say, or ballet or figure skating or, in more recent years, gymnastics. A friend of mine who lives in the Midwest has a daughter who became a serious figure skater as a little girl. On trips to New York, he sometimes told me about his experience as a skater daddy. He wasn't complaining, but a sort of haunted look came over him as he talked about getting up two hours early to take his daughter to some drafty rink for practice with her coach. He'd sit on a cold bench in the bleachers, trying to get a little work done before he took her to school and drove on to his office, where he arrived feeling as if he'd put in a day already. On weekends, there were the long drives to competitions. I could imagine my friend and his wife maintaining some pretense for a while that they liked the competing skaters — good sportsmanship and clean competition were, after all, some of the lessons that were supposed to make all of this worthwhile — and gradually becoming more open about the fact that they hated all the competing skaters, for whom they had created nicknames like "The Heifer" and "Smiley Face." I could imagine my friend, a man who would have unhesitatingly stepped in front of a speeding 18-wheeler to save his daughter from the slightest harm, sitting on the frigid benches of those practice arenas and realizing that his thoughts had turned to the possibility of the tiniest of hairline fractures — absolutely painless, of course — that would not interfere in the slightest with the ordinary movements of an active child but would, alas, put an end to his daughter's skating career.

Then I remember Ned Speller, which was about as close as we ever got to a systematic child-improvement regimen. "Perhaps you've heard of Ned Speller," I say to the inspector, who barely bothers to look up from his list. Ned Speller began as a way of doing something about Abigail's spelling. She was then in the lower grades at PS 3, a progressive and creative establishment that did not appear to concentrate much of its energy on such mundane matters as spelling. Her problem, of course, could have been genetic. The fact that my cousin Keith, from Salina, reached the finals of the Kansas state spelling bee seems to argue against that. On the other hand, I revealed around this time that I'd married Alice under the impression that she could spell "occurred" — although that was not specifically part of the discussion we had about getting married and may not have come out even if we had been subjected to one of those pre-marital counseling sessions that some states began to make mandatory thirty years or so later. At the time we got married, Alice was a college English teacher, and I simply assumed that her spelling knowledge would be, if not universal, at least complementary to mine; it turned out, though, that, despite having gone to school thirteen hundred miles apart, we were unable to spell the same words.

Someone knowledgeable about technology of the future could have told us that computer spell checks would make spelling an irrelevant skill by the time Abigail emerged from high school — although, as someone who sometimes writes about the goings-on in Washington, I began to have difficulty with spell checks as early as the Reagan administration, when it became obvious that they weren't programmed to recognize words like "wacko." Having been unaware during Abigail's childhood that such miracles as spell checks were imminent, I decided one summer that we should launch a small spelling project, sort of like Hickory Hill except for the absence of any Olympic champions to speak of. On the theory that Abigail would have more fun correcting my mistakes than having me correct hers, I wrote a one-page story every night about the adventures of a boy named Ned Speller, Abigail corrected the mistakes (sometimes mumbling "dumb Daddy-o" in a sort of singsong as she went), and Alice went over the corrections with Abigail. A couple of summers later, Abigail and I took turns writing about Ned Speller — I still made a lot of spelling errors — and a summer or two after that both Sarah and Alice got a turn in the round robin. In the first episode I wrote, Ned woke up one morning excited about the prospect of going to a fair. As the plot evolved over the next few summers, the girls would try to make progress toward the fair when they had control of the story, and the next night Alice or I would invent some sort of obstacle that would keep poor Ned from all that cotton candy.

For the first time since he had materialized in front of me, the inspector looks rather pleased. "I assume you still have copies of these stories," he says.

"Well, actually, I can't find them," I say. "They were definitely in one manila folder—I can still picture it exactly—but the last time I looked for it I couldn't seem to put my hand on it. I'm afraid our family's like that. For instance, when I say that one of us did a Ned Speller episode every night, I suppose I should have said, to be absolutely accurate, that 'every night' in the case of our family tends to mean every night that we remember to do it, not every *single* night, if you see what I mean."

The inspector seems unsympathetic. His expression is again severe, maybe even disapproving. "No other educational summer activities?" he asks, looking at his form. "No trips to Europe that included organized architectural tours? No trips made with the express purpose of improving the children's language skills? Under Methods of Tourism, what's this here about 'hanging around'?"

I consider telling the inspector some of the cultural advantages of hanging around. For instance, if you do come across a museum you've enjoyed—a museum devoted to the works of Fernand Léger, say, or to antique farm implements—you're allowed to go back the next day instead of moving on to the next museum. I decide against it. The inspector does not appear to be a man with a deep appreciation of farm implements. Also, I realize that I'm on the record about the motives behind that trip to France. In a travel book, I wrote, "I suppose I could say that we decided to take a house in the South of France for a month because it would give Abigail an opportunity to improve her French, but that would be like a newly rich businessman saying that he decided to buy a brand-new Cadillac El Dorado because a heavy car sticks to the road: it's true, but it's not the whole story."

Then, about the time I think my interview with the inspector has ended in ignominy, Alice speaks up. I hadn't even realized that she is able to see the inspector, who is, after all, a figment of my imagination. "Do the summer movies count?" she says. "Maybe the summer movies should count."

"Yes, maybe the summer movies should count," I say.

In the summer, we used to make movies — at first, silent movies with a narration added and eventually movie musicals. I suppose you could argue that the girls learned a lot about mushrooms, for instance, from *Yech: A Marvelous Mushroom Murder Mystery Musical Movie*, in which the visiting mushroom authority sings, "I can tell chanterelle yards away by the smell. I gobble boletus like French-fried potatoes, while categorizing morel." It's difficult, though, to put the summer movies in the category of a learning experience that would be acceptably focused for those who see childhood as a sort of cram course for adult life.

It occurs to me that I might pass off the summer movies as moral lessons. The bad guys, after all, tended to lose at the end. The murderer in *Yech: A Marvelous Mushroom Murder Mystery Musical Movie* was caught, although I can't remember offhand who it turned out to be. But the inspector is ready for that. He asks about certain lyrics. "For instance," he says, "this character described as 'the robber with the foxlike grin' persuades the characters described as 'two lovely little girls' to help steal a golden egg and then argues against their second thoughts by singing, 'Of course it's right to steal. Would you rather beg or borrow? Stealing's such a better deal.'" I offer to show him the movies to demonstrate to him that theft was not glorified. I tell him that he's welcome to bring in other people from his staff, or even friends and relatives, because we love showing the movies to anybody. He reminds me that I once wrote that people who show other people family movies or slides of the trip to Europe make me wonder if I am really an absolutist when it comes to the First Amendment after all.

"Well, anyway," I say lamely, "we had a good time making them."

"Good time!" the inspector says, sarcastically, and disappears.

5

Marriage, at Length

When one of our girls was in the first grade, the class made what I think was a fundamentally sound decision to buy a lizard for the classroom. Not having any particular obligations on the morning the lizard was going to be picked out, I volunteered to be among the parents who were to help herd the first-graders toward the obvious place in our neighborhood to make the purchase — a store that was then on Bleecker Street and went by the name of Exotic Aquatics. As we crossed Seventh Avenue on the way over to Exotic Aquatics, I took the hand of a little boy who had been pretty quiet as he walked along next to me for a couple of blocks. My usual icebreaker with a kid in that situation is a simple question: "Who is the meanest, nastiest, awfulest kid in your whole class?" I think of it as a relevant question. Also, it isn't hard to answer. I haven't met a kid yet who couldn't answer it, although one little boy I talked to in St. Louis mentioned five names instead of one. ("This kid's not in school," I said to his mother. "He's in a concentration camp.") Most kids answer right away. Usually, I regret to say, the nastiest, meanest, awfulest kid in the class is a boy. A remarkable percentage of the time, it's a boy named Jason. I don't know how to account for this, but if you're shopping around for a boy's name, it's something to keep in mind. Occasionally, I've met a kid—usually a little girl— who says immediately that there aren't any nasty, mean, awful children in her class. I wouldn't turn my back on a kid like that. The best answer I ever had to the question was also from a little girl—a particularly angelic-looking little girl of about five. We were sitting together on a couch in her living room. "Are you ready for the big question?" I asked.

"Sure," she said.

"O.K.," I said. "Of all the kids in your class, who is the nastiest, meanest, awfulest kid?"

She considered the question for just a moment, flashed her sweetest smile, and said, "I am."

I hadn't asked this little PS 3 boy the big question on the way to Exotic Aquatics. After all, my own daughter was in the class. I don't mean that I would have expected him to name her or that I would have tossed him out in the traffic if he had. Somehow, it just seemed inappropriate. Apparently trying out an icebreaker of his own—the sort of icebreaker you might need to carry out polite conversation with a strange grown-up— he looked up at me and said, "Are you divorced yet?"

"Not yet," I said.

I was pleased that at that point our conversation took a sudden swerve toward lizards—specifically, as I remember, to the subject of whether lizards bite and, if so, whether they are more likely to bite boys or girls. The next question I had expected

from a six-year-old I'd informed that I wasn't divorced yet—
"Why not?"—would have been difficult for me to answer, since
I didn't think my new friend was old enough to understand
how clever it had been of me, a decade before, to walk into
the right party.

Being asked by a six-year-old if I was divorced yet struck me
as a barometer of the spouse turnover in our neighborhood;
around that time I wrote about the possibility of our family
being put on the Gray Line Tour of the Village as the last
nuclear family in lower Manhattan. Still, some years later,
around the time of our twenty-fifth anniversary, it occurred to
us that we had among our friends any number of couples who'd
been married for a long time. Our anniversary falls in August,
while we're in Nova Scotia, and on the weekend of our twenty-
fifth a theater company in Parrsboro, a Bay of Fundy town
noted for its drastic tides, happened to be putting on a play we
wanted to see. As a tourist sight, even a tide that varies forty
feet or so from high to low is not suitable for the sort of tourist
who seeks instant gratification, since it takes six and a half hours
to go in or out. I later described the experience as a matter of
staring at the water from a lookout for a long time, until the
people standing next to you say something like "You folks from
Indiana?" We did acquire a sort of family folk phrase from that
trip: If we're wondering whether some couple has been together
for as long as twenty-five years, we say, "Have they been to
Parrsboro?"

It seems to me that the marriages we're familiar with that
have gone as far as Parrsboro are often unions of people with
different tastes and similar values. Among couples old enough
to have made it to Parrsboro some years ago, of course, differences in taste can often be traced to having grown up at a time

when little American girls and little American boys were raised in the expectation that they just naturally would have different interests and styles and ways of looking at things. It isn't simply that girls of that era were brought up to cook and boys weren't. Girls were brought up to appreciate meals as a daily ritual that's important enough to be observed even when nobody else is around. Once, after the girls had moved away, our friend Fats Goldberg happened to show up at our house around dinnertime on an evening I was out of town, and he found Alice eating alone. As he later described the scene to me, she had made herself a couple of perfect little lamb chops and a small green salad, and she was sitting in front of them at the dining-room table with a cloth napkin and, as I remember Fats's account, a glass of red wine. Alice doesn't believe that she was dining by candlelight; Fats may have added that as an adornment, along with a sprig of parsley on Alice's plate. The fat man was flabbergasted. He had never even realized that people who were having dinner alone might choose to sit down.

When I look back on what I've thought from time to time about the ways in which men and women are not alike, I find that I've been unable to give up the notion that it all gets down to one or two basic differences, planted deep in the chromosomes — although at various times I've had various ideas about what those one or two basic differences are. In the eighties, I know, I wrote a column that said, after the usual defensive maneuvering about how Alice was, in fact, much more capable of making sense out of a mathematical problem or a carburetor than I was, "I believe that in the spring female human beings get a deep biological urge to replace the living-room slipcovers. I'm not talking about something imposed by society — something that has to do with getting dollhouses for Christmas. I'm talking about something buried way down there in the chromosomes somewhere. And I'm talking about all women. I believe that in the spring Margaret Thatcher, on her way out of 10 Downing Street to deliver a stiff lecture to a group of poor people, will stop as she strides through the living room, turn to the Chancellor of the Exchequer and say, 'Doesn't it seem to you that the chintz on that armchair by the window is getting a bit tatty?' I believe that Sandra Day O'Connor's thoughts turn to slipcovers in the spring. So do the thoughts of female automobile mechanics and female physicists and female mud wrestlers. So, as it happens, do the thoughts of my wife."

Just a few years before that, though, I remember identifying the one chromosomal difference between males and females differently. When the girls were about nine and twelve, we went on a sort of amusement park tour, mainly to ride roller coasters. I had been presented with an opportunity to test the tips handed out by an organization called Roller Coaster Buffs International. It didn't take long to discover that Alice had never seen the appeal of roller coasters. In fact, she thought that the very existence of groups like Roller Coaster Buffs International was at least childish and maybe loony. As the girls and I stood in line for a roller coaster called the Loch Ness Monster, advertised as having a G-force of three point five, Alice even expressed some concern about whether the ride would be too frightening for a nine-year-old child. (As it turned out, Sarah's response to a ride on the Loch Ness Monster was "Too short and not scary enough." She'd had her eyes closed, of course. In those days, she was fearless as long as her eyes were closed. If no eye-opening had been necessary, Sarah at nine could have stood her ground in the face of a charge by a battalion of Chinese regulars. It strikes me now that we never thought of having her close her eyes and *then* take a bite of lobster.)

"They'll be fine," I said confidently as we reached the ticket booth. My confidence was based partly, I suppose, on the fact that I had no idea what "G-force" means, but also partly on the role an American father has traditionally played in roller-coaster situations. I know that it occurred to me during our roller-coaster adventures that when all the controversy was over about how male and female roles are played in this country — about what is buried in the chromosomes and what is culturally imposed — it will be agreed that the only difference between male and female behavior which is invariably and irrevocably in the nature of the beings is that in the face of a roller-coaster ride mothers make appeals for good sense and fathers say, "They'll be fine."

A dozen years later, on the other hand, I completely contradicted that conclusion in a poem I wrote on the subject of how Alice knows what she knows about fashion:

JUST HOW DO YOU SUPPOSE THAT ALICE KNOWS?

Just how do you suppose that Alice knows
So much about what's au courant in clothes?
You wouldn't really think that she's the sort
To know much more than whether skirts are short
Or long again, or somewhere in between.
She's surely not the sort who would be seen
In front-row seats at Paris fashion shows.
In fact, she looks at that sort down her nose.
For her to read a fashion mag would seem
As out of synch as reading Field & Stream.
Biographies are what she reads instead.
And yet, she has, in detail, in her head

Whose indigos are drawing ooh's and oh's.
Just how do you suppose that Alice knows?

We're leaving, and I'll ask her, once we've gone,
"What was that thing that whatzername had on?
It lacked a back. The front was sort of lined
With gauzy stuff. It seemed to be the kind
Of frock that might be worn by Uncle Meyer
If he played Blanche in Streetcar Named Desire."
And Alice knows. She knows just who designed
The rag and why some folks are of a mind
To buy this shmatameister's frilly things
For what a small Brancusi usually brings.
She knows which dress is newly chic this year
Although it looked like antique fishing gear.
I'm stunned, as if she'd talked in Urdu prose.
Just how do you suppose that Alice knows?

She gets no E-mail info on design.
(She's au courant, but, so far, not on-line.)
No fashion maven tells her what is kitsch.
She goes to no symposium at which
She learns why some designer's models pose
As Navajos or folks from UFOs.
I know that women have no special gene
Providing knowledge of the fashion scene,
The way that men all have, without a doubt,
The chromosome for garbage-taking-out.
And yet she's fashion-conscious to her toes.
Does she divine these things? Does she osmose
What's in the air concerning hose and bows?
Just how do you suppose that Alice knows?

Even after accounting for gender differences, it's not always easy to distinguish between tastes and values. How about, for instance, a marriage between a woman who eats mainly salads and a man who is what used to be called strictly a meat-and-potatoes guy? There was a time when that difference would have been considered literally a matter of taste. The wife, who might have preferred no more than a cottage cheese and fruit plate for dinner, would have been conscious of her husband's need to stoke up with a pound or so of red meat every night in the same way she'd be conscious of his preference for sleeping with the windows open rather than closed. These days, though, watching him devour what amounts to a cholesterol bomb, she has to wonder whether she is married to the sort of man so fundamentally cavalier that he is willing to toy with his health despite the responsibilities he has to his family. Her husband might wonder, as he chews his steak, whether the pile of lettuce on the plate in front of his wife is meant as a judgment of him for being callous enough to eat one of God's creatures or merely as a way of saying that he is complicit in the destruction of the Amazon rain forest by cattle ranchers. The clash of values might be deep enough to impair the digestion of both parties.

For a magazine assignment not long after the election between Bill Clinton and George Bush, Alice and I went to Virginia to have a casual Sunday supper with James Carville and Mary Matalin, two people who had become known for such passionate commitment to the opposing political values they had worked for in the campaign that some people saw their marriage as analogous to the marriage of, say, a deeply committed internist and a devout Christian Scientist—the sort of union you could imagine being shaken to its foundations by a simple "Did you have a nice day at the office, dear?" The Car-ville-Matalins said that at home they simply avoided the subject of politics. They preferred to see themselves as simply one among many married couples who avoid one sort of touchy subject or another—maybe her family or his boss or religion or money or, now and then, politics. If married couples all had identical political values, after all, there would be no such thing as "the gender gap," and the presidential election of 1996 might have put Robert Dole in the White House.

Apparently, James and Mary really were able to avoid con-tentious political issues pretty well, at least when Alice wasn't present. I don't mean that Alice had gone to their house in-tending to cause trouble; she'd met James and Mary once be-fore, and had taken an instant liking to both of them. I only mean that, in my experience, Alice has an almost instinctual attraction for avoided subjects. Once, when we had dinner in Chinatown with some friends and an out-of-town guest of theirs who had been described to us as a sugar baron, I counted three times that Alice's conversation, circling in from completely un-related subjects, came around to matters reflecting on the mor-bid connection between sugar and rotten teeth. By the time coffee came, the sugar baron looked as if he would find it a relief to discuss diabetes for a while.

At the Carville-Matalin residence, we sat in the kitchen, while James, with Mary's assistance and constructive criticism, fixed dinner. James is a serious preparer of the southern Loui-siana specialties he grew up eating, and he seemed to follow the Louisiana tradition of telling the guests how spectacular some dish like the tomato-and-okra stew was going to be so that the bliss of the first bite would not come as the sort of shock that could cause them to swoon right at the table. We would all be cheerfully discussing, say, Cajun boudin, when, somehow following naturally from something Alice had said, we'd find ourselves in a heated discussion of health care policy. James would be using some unkind words to describe Mary's political allies and Mary would be referring to James as a "redistributionist." In a few moments, the storm would pass, and Mary would be telling James that the tomato-and-okra stew was his personal best. I realized that James had been fortunate enough to find someone who is compatible with him in the kitchen. After all, he might have fallen for someone whose idea of a casual Sunday supper revolved around goat cheese and radicchio. When you contemplate the difference between James Carville and someone like that—someone of fundamentally different values, if I may say so—a deep philosophical disagreement about deficit spending pales in comparison.

Alice and I don't have serious political differences, although I have never officially signed on to either one of her major initiatives in the area of economics and tax policy—what I've described in columns as Alice's Law of Compensatory Cash Flow, which holds that any money not spent on a luxury you can't afford should be treated as windfall income, and the Alice Tax, a proposal that Mary Matalin would consider redistributionist in the extreme. "To state the provisions of the Alice Tax simply, which is the only way Alice allows them to be stated," I've written, "it calls for this: after a certain level of income, the government would simply take everything. Alice believes that at a certain point an annual income is simply more than anybody could possibly need for even a lavish style of living. She is willing to discuss what that point is. In her more flexible moments, she is even willing to listen to arguments about which side of the line a style of living that included, say, a large oceangoing boat should fall on. But she insists that there is such a thing as enough — a point of view that separates her from, say, the United States Senate."

We do differ in a number of tastes. For instance, I've acknowledged publicly that Alice adores scenery and I am indifferent to scenery. In Nova Scotia, there are two routes for the fifteen- or twenty-minute drive from our house to the nearest town large enough to have a supermarket or a drugstore. The route Alice takes every time is what she calls the pretty way and I call the long way. My way — what I refer to as the short way — is referred to by Alice as the ugly way. She says the ugly way is no shorter than the pretty way. Alice has more tolerance than I do for the polished-silver restaurants I refer to as sherbet-in-the-middle joints, and she loves stopping late in the afternoon for tea; I think of tea as something your mother made you drink when you were kept home from school with a bad cold. Alice and I also have some differences when it comes to interior design, a good example being her underappreciation for my American Hereford Association poster. I suppose we must have different tastes in men's clothing; that's the only way I can account for the number of times she has asked me, as we're about to leave the house, "Is that the jacket you're going to wear?" We have different tastes in movies. Those may be summed up by the fact that the clip-clop sound that horses make in pulling the carriages that always appear in those faithful adaptations of early-nineteenth-century novels Alice loves tends to put me to sleep. We also have differing notions on how important it is for people who are watching a movie to monitor its level of verisimilitude — to call attention to the fact, for instance, that the defense attorney who is questioning the witness would not actually be allowed to say what he is saying in a real court of law.

On that division, Alice can be identified as the one who is saying, "Shhhhhhh."

Occasionally, I've read an article reporting that one of the differences between us can be a serious threat to a marriage. I think we had already been to Parrsboro when I read that about having widely varying sleeping schedules. Reading in bed at about nine-thirty one evening, I learned of a study in the *Journal of Marital and Family Therapy* that discussed the difficulties that can arise in a marriage between a night person and a day person. I was going to ask Alice for her views on this subject, but before I could do that I fell asleep. As my eyes closed, it occurred to me that I could ask her in the morning, but, as usual, she was still sleeping when I got up. "Oh, well," I thought. "It probably wasn't very important anyway."

That morning, as I was bustling around, occasionally wondering how Alice could stand to waste the best part of the day, I thought of a subject that I'd like to see treated in the *Journal of Marital and Family Therapy*: the difficulties that can arise in a marriage between a person who doesn't like asparagus and a person who can't believe that anybody could not like asparagus. The researchers, I figured, could do their fieldwork at our house. As far as I can gather from the occasional family-dynamics study that makes the newspaper, serious researchers have pretty much ignored the asparagus situation. In general, they don't seem to deal much with the phenomenon of non-believing—the phenomenon we see reflected in a wife who, for example, can't believe that she, the onetime homecoming queen of Holafield Unified High School, could possibly be married to the crude slob who appears to be her husband.

When it comes to the question of someone in a marriage not being able to believe that her spouse does not like asparagus, I think what the researchers would find is that there are stages, the first one being what some might call denial and some others might call hard-of-hearing. You can tell if you're in that stage when the following conversation takes place at the dinner table during a meal that includes asparagus:

Wife: Isn't this asparagus absolutely delicious!

Husband: Actually, I've never particularly cared for asparagus.

Wife: This is really the time of year for fresh asparagus. I just hope it isn't all gone before I can get to the store tomorrow and buy some more.

At one point, of course, Abigail and Sarah got old enough to notice that I wasn't wolfing down my asparagus. I can't remember the tip-off phrase, but it was something like "How come Daddy doesn't have to finish his vegetables? Don't those places where there are starving children have starving grown-ups too?"

"Actually," I said as all eyes turned my way, "I've never particularly cared for asparagus."

At that moment, the hard-of-hearing stage ended. Alice heard me. She seemed absolutely flabbergasted. I might as well have said, "Oh, by the way, Alice, I meant to tell you years ago: this right leg of mine that seems absolutely natural is actually made of a durable but quite flexible plastic alloy."

"I can't believe anybody could not like fresh asparagus," Alice said.

The girls, who had been pushing their asparagus around as if hoping against hope that they might come across a slot in the plate it would fall through, let that one ride. They sat there silently while we entered what the researchers would call the second stage — overt, flat-out nonbelieving. For a few years after that, at the time of year when fresh asparagus became available, Alice would simply look at me, shake her head sadly and say, "I can't believe it." Eventually, she began to believe it, but she never retreated from the position that I am the only person in the world who does not like fresh asparagus—stage three. "It's too bad we can't have fresh asparagus," she said one afternoon, when we were discussing what we might serve some friends who were coming to our house for dinner. "Everybody else loves it."

It obviously isn't difficult to adjust to something like differing views of asparagus; we had that one sorted out in just ten or twelve years. It isn't difficult to adjust to any difference, as long as it's a difference that rests on taste or style or personality. In Nova Scotia, when we go into town together, I sometimes find myself driving the route that Alice considers the pretty way—although I've never gone so far as to admit that it's no longer than the short way. (Marriage may be compromise, but it is not capitulation.) In New York, Alice often finds that an evening when I'm out of town is a convenient time to rent the video of what we generally refer to around our house as a sissy movie. Adjusting to differences in values would be another matter. After the girls were grown, Alice decided that, in retrospect, we did have a child-rearing policy, similar to the policy used by Chinatown parents in that study I'd read about: we were lenient about small matters and strict about large ones. We never had to talk about which were which.

6

Diaper Daddy

Long after Abigail and Sarah were grown, the White House and a number of experts on child development launched a program to impress upon parents how much mental development goes on during a child's earliest years. The experts emphasized that for developmental purposes it is vital to talk to infants who are only weeks old and who at first glance don't strike you as the sort of folks you'd fall into a conversation with. I was all for the program, of course, but it did present a problem for those of us whose children hadn't been babies for some time: Although I have a hazy memory of what my kids were like when they were tiny, I can't for the life of me remember what I said to them.

That is particularly true of what are now commonly referred to as the vital first few months of life. At the time, I didn't realize that they were in the vital first few months of life. If I had, I would have taken notes. A lot of the conversations I had with our girls when they were that age seemed to take place in the wee hours of the morning, at a time when I was so sleepy that I wasn't quite certain whether I was really awake or simply having another diaper dream. (I can't remember the specifics of a diaper dream either. It might have been similar to one of those classic anxiety dreams, in which you haven't prepared for the exam or can't find your ticket for the flight or can't seem to make it to the airport in the first place, except this time you've run out of diapers.) When one of our babies woke up before dawn, did I recite *The Canterbury Tales* to her in a way that stimulated the bejesus out of her brain circuitry or did I just mutter unintelligibly, "Where the hell did she throw the bottle now?" I can't claim to be certain about that. At this point, it isn't even easy to remember precisely what I said to the girls when they were teenagers. After the news of the Heaven's Gate mass suicide broke in the press, at a time when both of my daughters were well past voting age, I was tempted to get in touch with both of them and say, "We did remember to tell you not to join any cults, didn't we?"

According to what the latest research indicates about a child's earliest years, it's important to try to recall what I said in those first months. It's important to face the uncomfortable possibility that I might not have said enough. One scientific report quoted at the White House Conference on Early Childhood Development and Learning concluded that brain synapses—connections between brain cells—are formed before the age of three, and that those unformed by then are eliminated. As I interpreted that finding, my daughters could be walking around with less than their fair share of brain synapses simply because some nights when I was making a diaper run at 4 a.m. I was too tired to manage at least a simple "Hiya, kid. What's new?"

This business about synapses struck me as the sort of finding that could have been designed to add to the concerns of those older parents who already spend some uncomfortable time, while trying to fall asleep at night, thinking of ways that they may have shortchanged their children. Here is an entirely new subject, pushing aside old chestnuts like whether that really was the right summer camp or whether the purchase of the guitar might have been to blame for everything that followed. Now, as they toss and turn, they can envision their children trying to compete in a global economy with reduced brainpower. Even worse, the child might have read about the White House conference himself, and would therefore know whose fault it is every time he hands in the report without remembering to include the numbers that the boss specifically asked for.

Did I have to worry about one of my daughters being provoked by news of the White House conference to cast blame on her father for being an irresponsibly uncommunicative brute during those early-morning encounters? They had not previously indulged in those sorts of accusations. It would have been more characteristic for them to say, "There wasn't any reason to worry about our reading the White House report, Daddy. With all the eliminated synapses we have, we probably wouldn't have understood it anyway."

To which I would have replied, characteristically, "I'll make the jokes in this family." I find it helpful to make that point fairly regularly, even now that they're grown.

In a way, I suppose, the girls are the best source on what was or wasn't said during our earliest conversations. Unlike me, after all, they were wide awake; nobody could have made that much noise while asleep. "You don't happen to recall hearing anything in those days about pilgrims wending their way to Canterbury, do you?" I thought about asking one of them.

"Actually, Daddy," she'd probably say, "I think you might have used some bad language when you were having trouble with the diaper pins."

It was starting to come back to me. When trying to lull them back to sleep, I remembered, I hadn't recited *The Canterbury Tales*; I had sung an old World War II ditty called "If I Had It to Do All Over Again, I'd Do It All Over You." It had seemed more appropriate at the time.

In fact, they both seem to have an abundant supply of synapses — maybe even a plethora, a surfeit, an overabundance. It's always possible that the bad language was good for the brain circuitry — a little jolt to get those brain cells jumping. A couple of years after Abigail got out of college, she and I took a trip to Veracruz together. We spent our evenings sitting in one of the cafés under the portals of the city square, where strolling entrepreneurs offered not only peanuts or hammocks or wooden statuary or earrings or model ships or a serenade but, rather to my surprise, an electric shock. According to a man carrying equipment that looked alarmingly like jumper cables, the shock would pretty much take care of whatever happened to be ailing you. At the time, I was not convinced. I've never been a believer in unorthodox treatments; my idea of alternative medicine is a doctor who didn't go to Johns Hopkins. After I read about the White House conference on early childhood development, though, I began to wonder. The parallel with a jolt of blue language to the brain circuitry is obvious.

I don't doubt that I had some harsh words to say about diaper pins during those changing episodes that are now so blurry in my mind. I hated diaper pins, partly because they seemed to be such a dangerous instrument for such a routine task. I kept thinking, "Why am I risking the possibility of poking a hole into this little baby just to change her diapers?" Some years later, in fact, I may have said that if Pampers with tabs for fastening had been on the market when our girls were babies we would have had many more children. Someone had remarked that we had more or less the number of children the demographic studies showed as typical, and I remember replying, "What kept the number down was diaper pins." Paper diapers—not, at first, with tabs on them for closing—appeared right around the time Abigail did. In some places, they remained hard to get until she was at the point of not needing them. I remember traveling to Nova Scotia in the first summer of Abigail's life with a case of Pampers on the roof rack of the car, hoping that the Canadian customs inspector was someone who'd had enough late-night experience with babies to be sympathetic. In London the next summer, I remember driving to obscure neighborhoods on the rumor that some eccentric pharmacy was stocking an oddly shaped but still adequate English version.

The birth of Abigail also roughly coincided with the blossoming of the environmental movement. Despite the publication of a few shockers like *Silent Spring*, environmentalists had been almost invisible before then except for the occasional appearance in the press of people who seemed mainly interested in keeping tacky developments away from the views available from their summer-house porches. When Abigail was born, concern about the environment was not yet so acute that each new product was weighed for its impact on landfills and air quality and the ozone layer and our supply of irreplaceable fossil fuels. Eventually, though, there was a spirited public debate about whether paper diapers were an environmentally sound alternative to cloth diapers, considering not only how many trees had to be chopped down to keep one baby's bottom dry but how much landfill had to be used for disposal. I was pleased that a case was made for paper diapers causing no more harm to the environment than the constant recycling of cloth diapers, but I was pleased only in the sense that a farmer in southwestern France would presumably be pleased to hear the news that the red wine he accepts as one of life's routine pleasures could be useful in fighting off such physical problems as clogged arteries: he was going to drink it anyway.

When it was revealed, years later, that the environmental arguments in favor of paper diapers were mainly a product of a huge public-relations campaign carried on by the companies that controlled the paper-diaper market, I was not able to work up my usual outrage against corporate attempts at thought control. Once tabs became available on paper diapers, making diaper pins obsolete, we were not interested in anti-Pampers arguments based on the environment or on anything else. At that point, if disposable diapers had been declared illegal on environmental grounds, I might have developed a foreign source or sought out a bootlegger who diversified his inventory with Pampers.

So I did use Pampers with tabs after all. They must have been on the market when our girls were babies, at least by the time Sarah came along. If diaper pins were no longer a factor in our lives, then why didn't we have any more children? Could I have diaper pins confused in my mind with buttons and zippers on snowsuits? I know that after our daughters were grown someone said to me that there had to be a lot about having small children around that we were happy to be finished with, and I distinctly remember saying that all I could think of offhand was snowsuits. I didn't really enjoy buttoning all those buttons and zipping all those zippers, and then, ten minutes later, unbuttoning all those buttons and unzipping all those zippers, and then starting all over again. I suppose we could have moved to the Sun Belt, but for people who weren't even willing to move to the suburbs, moving to the Sun Belt was never a realistic option. (Whoever I was talking to informed me, of course, that snowsuits have Velcro on them now, so you don't have to button all those buttons and zip up all those zippers.) So maybe what I said about having the average number of children was "What kept the number down was buttons and zippers on snowsuits."

Whether it was snowsuits or diaper pins, what I was getting at is the importance of what you might call baby technology. By chance, our children arrived during a period of enormous technological advances in the care of babies; Abigail and Sarah were like a couple of natural-born manufacturers wandering into Birmingham or Leeds from the boondocks just in time for the industrial revolution. Disposable diapers were introduced. Someone invented umbrella strollers—the sort that fold up into something not much larger than a shooting stick. The Jolly Jumper, a sort of seat on springs that hung in a doorjamb, went on sale. The breakthrough baby carrier, the Snugli, gradually came on the market. When Abigail was born, a friend gave us a Snugli, which was then available only through the mail from Snugli headquarters in Colorado—a rare item that bound its owners into a loose community, like early drivers of Volkswagen Beetles.

As new parents, caught up in the world of babies, we were thrilled by the advances in baby technology. When Abigail was about five months old, Alice and I went to a conference in New Orleans, and Alice spotted a woman carrying a baby in a

Snugli. Approaching the woman to exchange Snugli experiences, Alice found herself talking to the person who had designed and marketed the Snugli—the person known in our house as the Snugli Lady. We learned that as a Peace Corps volunteer the Snugli Lady had observed the way African women carried babies on their chests as they went about their daily chores, and had adapted the contraption to produce an American baby carrier. The sense of awe we felt at meeting the actual Snugli Lady was not matched for several years, until we were introduced to the person who had actually written "It Isn't Easy Being Green," the Kermit the Frog classic.

The war stories Snugli owners exchanged were often about well-meaning citizens who approached to suggest that the child sleeping peacefully in the sort of cocoon a fully zipped Snugli formed on the parent's chest might not be able to breathe. I seemed to attract a lot more breathing inspectors than Alice did. It was probably still unusual in those days to see a man walking through the supermarket in the middle of a workday with a baby strapped to his chest, and, given the unfamiliarity of the Snugli, the first glance tended to linger. New Yorkers are, of course, famously reluctant to approach a person who seems to be acting oddly. Partly, they feel the need to maintain the imaginary little isolation booth they wear as protection against all of those other people, and partly they don't want to acknowledge that there is anything they haven't seen at least once. If a 300-pound man costumed as Eleanor of Aquitaine walked on a New York subway carrying both an attaché case and a rib roast, the other passengers might glance up for a second, but then they'd go back to their tabloids. If you asked one of them why he didn't seem to be registering any sort of reaction to such a sight, he'd say, "Hey, whadaya—kidding? I seen a million guys like that. You think I'm some kinda farmer or something?" But, as the guests from abroad who left their babies unattended outside the bar found out, the normal New York reluctance to get involved tends to evaporate under the possibility that a child is in danger. Any number of times, an alarmed citizen, almost always a woman, approached me while I was carrying Abigail in the Snugli and asked if I was absolutely certain that the baby could breathe in there.

In the beginning, I responded in a friendly enough way. After all, I have similar instincts. There are times when I have to restrain myself from approaching complete strangers on the street and saying something like "Don't you think you ought to button up the baby's jacket, with this wind?" or "I wonder if you'd mind if I took that sharp stick out of your little boy's hand before he pokes himself in the eye." I'd actually considered, at one point, the chances of passing a New York City ordinance prohibiting tables with sharp corners. In the beginning of my Snugli questioning, I told the concerned citizens who approached me that I appreciated their interest, but wanted to assure them that there was actually nothing to worry about: the carrier was designed so the baby could fit in comfortably and safely. Babies carried in Snuglis tended to be lulled to sleep by the parent's heartbeat, much the way babies are lulled to sleep by the sound and motion of a car. Sometimes, I even told the story of the Snugli Lady in Africa, and how the sewing of Snuglis had become a sort of cottage industry for the church friends of the Snugli Lady's mother. After a while, though, I got tired of the inquiries. I'd say something like "She can breathe" and leave it at that. At times, I should admit, I said "She can breathe" in a tone that might have been considered brusque. Finally, I changed tactics completely. I started saying, in a friendly voice, "It's not a baby. It's only a doll." That seemed to satisfy them; there's no need for a doll to breathe. They'd nod and walk away, obviously relieved. After four or five paces they'd usually pause for a moment, apparently beginning to wonder what a full-grown man was doing walking up and down the aisles of the Daitch-Shopwell supermarket with a doll strapped to his chest.

The changes in baby-care equipment that took place in that era were accompanied by changing ideas about who in the family would be using it. Some fathers, I suppose, did not feel as strongly as I did about preferring one sort of diaper over another because diapering was not among their household tasks. The duty roster for such tasks varied a lot from family to family, as I suppose it still does. As feminism raised questions about the traditional split-up of family duties, who was and who wasn't involved in diapering became a subject of discussion among people we knew. Around our house, the way we indicated someone who was no stranger to the changing table was to say, "He's checked out on diapers." I liked the way it sounded. It made being a practiced nappy-swapper sound sort of like having a security clearance. We found ourselves saying, "Is Mac checked out?" or "Mary says that Marty is completely checked out."

So why was I checked out from the start? For one thing, I was, unlike most fathers, usually on the premises. I had to be out of town regularly to report stories, so when I was in New York I worked mainly at home. If writers who work at home were asked why I became checked out on diapers, they would be drawn to a simple theory: anything can serve as a procrastination device. These are writers who have always sharpened a lot of pencils before they got to work and didn't sharpen any fewer when they began working completely on a word processor. Some of them are people who have put off their work because they've convinced themselves that, even though it's only November, they'd better get a start on comparison-shopping air-conditioning units. I'm sure they could easily envision me responding to the first cries of a wet baby by leaping from my desk—where a paragraph that was, alas, absolutely necessary to the narrative hadn't been going well at all—and shouting, "I'll get this one, honey," as I walked purposefully toward the crib.

It would be foolish for a writer to deny that procrastination plays some role in almost anything he does around the house, but there were other factors. For one thing, anyone who wants to have something to do with an infant has limited options. When a baby is a couple of weeks or a couple of months old, there aren't many ways to interact with her. You can hold her or feed her or bathe her or try to get her to sleep or change her diapers. Teaching her tennis or doing a little horseback riding together would not be among the options. By the time our daughters were grown, sharing child-care duties was so common that they would never have thought to ask me why I hadn't considered following my father's policy of leaving diaper changing to females. If they had, I suppose I would have told them that even in those days a forward-looking male knew that if he didn't participate in that elementary aspect of baby care he might be robbing himself of the opportunity to say, during a stressful family conversation fifteen or twenty years down the road, "I changed your *diapers!*"

For twenty years or so, I didn't think much about the issue of who was or wasn't checked out. I had my suspicions, of course—sometimes I would meet a guy whose entire attitude led me to believe he wasn't checked out—but I didn't inquire. Then I became aware of a significant change in American society. I'm afraid that when I made this discovery I was in a men's room. This was just off Interstate 84, east of Hartford. Driving toward Nova Scotia, Alice and I had stopped at some sort of franchise restaurant. As I was about to leave the men's room, I glanced at an unfamiliar object on the wall and suddenly realized that it was a pull-down diaper-changing table. In the men's room!

My first thought was that the presence of a diaper-changing table in the men's room might have been a fluke. It might have reflected a gesture by a single corporation, made because the vice president of ancillary customer services happened to be a modern woman or happened to be what Abigail used to call a snag—a college acronym that stood for sensitive New Age guy. A snag was the sort of guy who went on pro-choice marches and took a lot of courses in the women's studies department and was regularly moved to tears by movies. Abigail used to say that she didn't like going to the movies with a snag she knew because you couldn't hear the dialogue over the sniffling. The accidental presence of a snag somewhere in middle management could, I suppose, explain the presence of a changing table in the men's room. Evidence against this theory presented itself that very day in a men's room a few hours down the road and, not long after that, in a men's room on a car ferry. At that point, I heard myself mumbling, "It's here, guys. It's here."

The next time I spotted a changing table it had a logo on it that showed a picture of a koala and the legend Koala Bear Kare. My friend Pierre had been visiting us in Nova Scotia, and I'd driven him to the airport to get a plane home. We walked into the men's room at the airport together. He saw Koala Bear

Kare at the same time I did. He didn't seem alarmed. Pierre's children, like my children, were grown by then.

I nodded toward Koala Bear Kare. "I assume you're checked out," I said.

"Oh, sure," he said. "And I know you're checked out."

"Yes, of course," I said.

"I'm checked out on changing diapers," Pierre said. "But I might have a little trouble figuring out how to get that gizmo down out of the wall."

"On the other hand," I said, "it seems to me that there was a time when you were concerned about your ability to master a dishwashing machine. And now you're noted for glassware that twinkles with that sparkling shine."

I would think that most modern fathers are checked out. But I would also think that a lot of modern fathers—some snags among them—have considered themselves more or less off duty when the family's eating out. In fact, it wouldn't surprise me if some of them had stood in front of the mirror now and then, polishing the gesture they use in public when the baby is in obvious need of changing—a sort of apologetic shrug, communicating at the same time both regret at not being able to shoulder the burden this time and helplessness in the face of a world organized to assign changing tables only to women's rooms.

If my experience in those New England men's rooms is any guide, the world is no longer organized that way. I can't help wondering how this will affect families. I can't help wondering how it will affect men's rooms. Traditionally, the atmosphere in men's rooms is a little—well, edgy. Will the presence of a cooing baby being powdered loosen things up? Will strangers now stop by the Koala Bear Kare table, say something like

"Cute little booger," and fall into a conversation about diaper-rash remedies?

I also couldn't help wondering why I hadn't heard about this before. I try to keep up. Is it possible that men—presumably the only people who use men's rooms—have been consciously keeping mum about the availability of changing tables? If so, I hope they are not laboring under the misapprehension that there is a realistic possibility of keeping this secret. What they ought to be doing is polishing a new gesture—a cheerful smile that comes along with saying, "Let me get this one, honey. You finish your fajita while it's still hot." Because it's here, guys. It's here.

7

Memories of an Ax Murderer

Halloween is my holiday. Living in New York, I've had plenty of other holidays to choose from. In New York, alternate-side-of-the-street-parking regulations are suspended every year for the Feast of the Ascension and Sh'mini Asereth and Id al-Adha, the Muslim Feast of Sacrifice. There are people in my neighborhood who are specialists in celebrating the Feast Day of St. Anthony. There are parts of New York—not just Chinatown, in lower Manhattan, but an entirely separate Chinese neighborhood in Queens—where people stop whatever they're doing in February to celebrate Chinese New Year. In New York, it is common for several thousand people to turn out into the streets for a celebration of a holiday that people in most other parts of the country have never heard of. It wouldn't surprise me to learn that there is someone in Borough Park or Williamsburg known among his friends and acquaintances as "a Tisha B'Ov sort of guy." There are huge parades on Fifth Avenue for the national days of any number of countries — on Sundays, usually, because the Italians and the Irish are the only people who ever amassed enough clout to close Fifth Avenue for a parade on a weekday. There are New Yorkers who would never dream of being out of town on the day when their heritage is celebrated — the day marking the liberation of Greece or the unification of Germany or the birthday of Sun Yat-sen. I'm always in town for Halloween.

Halloween was not a major event during my childhood. I mainly remember prowling the neighborhood with a couple of other wannabe miscreants, talking about all the windows we were going to soap and garbage cans we were going to overturn and car horns we were going to stick. At the end of the evening, after inflicting negligible damage, we'd retreat to our homes muttering excuses, like a highly trained Special Forces unit that had been unable to find any enemy installations to destroy in the dark of night. My intense interest in Halloween certainly started when Abigail and Sarah were of grade school age, but the extent to which it was fueled by their presence has, over the years, been the subject of some debate among our friends. There is, of course, a theory that I began a vigorous celebration of Halloween because my daughters enjoyed it. There is also a theory that I used my daughters as an excuse to celebrate Halloween — a theory resting on the belief that my predilection for wearing foolish masks surpasses fatherhood.

When the girls were children, these speculations about my motives often seemed to take place during the week leading up to Halloween, as I frantically prepared for the big night while many of our adult friends were so oblivious of the impending celebration that they could only stare at me blankly when I said, "What are you going as?" The subject would sometimes be raised when a friend phoned to talk to me and Alice said something like "He's in the basement making sure the witch piñata is still in good enough shape to hang out the window" or "He's upstairs trying to decide whether the evil-old-man mask goes better with his panama hat or his Stewart Granger great-white-hunter hat."

There is a third way to account for the enthusiasm I displayed in celebrating Halloween with the girls—the long-established role of a father in passing on cultural traditions to the next generation. The responsibility rested particularly heavily on my shoulders in this case, because Alice's attitude toward Halloween has always bordered on the blasé. Alice is fond of Christmas. I have finally admitted to Alice, reluctantly, that I look forward to Christmas Day at our house, but the general five-week public celebration (if that's the word) provokes in me an otherwise dormant yearning to emigrate to someplace like Saudi Arabia. In fact, I once published a poem, presented as a sort of substitute for Bing Crosby's rendition of "White Christmas," that included among its choruses

> I'd like to spend next Christmas in Rangoon
> Or anyplace where Christmas is as noisy
> As Buddhist holidays might be in Boise.
> Next Christmas comes around again so soon.
> I long to hear Der Bingle smoothly croon
> "I'm dreaming of a Christmas in Rangoon"—
> Or someplace you won't hear the Christmas story,
> And reindeer's something eaten cacciatore.

In terms of national holidays, in other words, it's a mixed marriage. As a result, Alice and I have always engaged in one of those quiet struggles common to marriages of varying cultural emphasis. If I hadn't been there to hold up my end on Halloween when Abigail and Sarah were small, I suppose the possibility existed that the girls could have found themselves spending October 31 inventorying Christmas tree ornaments, pausing now and then to hand out tiny "Joyeux Noël" wreaths to the trick-or-treaters.

Fortunately, the Village is, among New York neighborhoods, particularly suited by spirit and architecture to Halloween celebrations. On my block in late October the response of an adult to being asked "What are you going as?" might be, instead of a blank look, a description of, say, a Day of the Dead costume, perhaps with a more detailed explanation of the symbolism than you were actually counting on. In fact, a lot of Villagers do not require a national holiday or even a Saturday night to dress in what people somewhere else might consider a costume. I've always thought that, at any time of year, about 10 percent of the people walking around the Village would be stopped by the police if they were in most American cities, and another 10 or 15 percent would at least be interviewed by the local TV news.

A lot of residential buildings in the Village are one- or two-family brownstones rather than those massive New York high-rises that can each hold approximately as many families as live in Terre Haute. I like to think that I would have done my best to pass on the more important cultural values of our society to my daughters no matter what neighborhood they grew up in, but, having been raised in the Midwest, where people tend to live in houses, I know that I would have found trick-or-treating in an Upper East Side high-rise an experience more bizarre than any of the costumes worn in the Village. "Who shall I say is calling?" I can imagine the doorman saying, as he stares icily at Sarah in her Winnie the Pooh costume and at Abigail pretending with some success to be a kangaroo and finally at me. I happen to be wearing a mask that has an unfortunate tendency to bring to people's minds any buried fears they may have had concerning ax murderers.

On the Halloween just after Abigail turned seven, when Sarah was about three and a half, we were walking down Seventh Avenue early in the evening with the thought of making a second strike at one of our most lucrative trick-or-treat targets—Ken and Eve's corner store, or what we then called the Bubble Gum Store. At the time, Ken and Eve were a young couple who ran a consciously old-fashioned establishment around the corner from our house—nothing more than a tiny, crowded room with a worn linoleum floor and a marble counter that had been placed toward the rear, so that the customers tended to collect in the center of the store rather than to pause briefly at the cash register to pay for their cat food or roast beef sandwich on the way out. Ken and Eve called most of the customers by name, and the conversation often drew in anyone who just happened to be standing in front of the counter waiting to pay for a quart of milk or searching among the canned goods along the wall for the right soup. Some of the customers had been introduced by Ken, who (sometimes as a disembodied voice from behind the meat-slicing machine) had a habit of saying, "Hey, you two might as well know each other—you're neighbors." The store had a rocking chair, which was often occupied, and a selection of homemade cookies and three or four antique but beautifully functioning gum-ball machines. Abigail and Sarah loved the Bubble Gum Store. Ken and Eve eventually transformed it into a restaurant—a place that had an astonishing array of dishes, including such rarities as Egyptian Burrito and White Trash Hash and Post-Modern Turkey Sandwich, and a policy of allowing a customer who had ordered a spicy dish to designate degree of hotness from one to ten (although one waitress refused, on humanitarian grounds, to accept a designation higher than six). Abigail and Sarah loved the restaurant, too; they continue to think of it as more or less an extension of our kitchen.

When Ken and Eve's was still the Bubble Gum Store, trick-or-treaters knew that it had the best supply of candy in the neighborhood. Ken and Eve actually carried a wide variety of sweets in their inventory, and they were also the sort of people who understood that, whatever your policy on nutrition happened to be during the rest of the year, giving trick-or-treaters apples or granola or mung bean crackers or the sort of candy that consists of soy waste sweetened with fruit juice amounts to finklike behavior. As we walked down Seventh Avenue toward the Bubble Gum Store, I changed my mask; in those days, difficulty in choosing among the various possibilities sometimes resulted in my going out with two or even three masks. I may have been entertaining a little fantasy about our not being recognized by Ken and Eve as repeaters.

Around Sheridan Square, I began to hear a band playing. The music grew closer and closer. It was not marching-band music. It was the sort of music I associate with plays by Bertolt Brecht. Suddenly, a parade streamed across Seventh Avenue in front of us. There seemed to be two or three hundred marchers—almost all of them, adults and children alike, in costume. There were also creatures beyond the costuming skill of even the most devout amateur Halloween celebrant. We were passed by a turn-of-the-century dandy at least ten feet tall, with a huge face made out of something like papier-mâché. He was in the company of a floozy even larger and funnier. A dozen marchers armed with tall bamboo poles held aloft a forty-foot serpent that bobbed and danced through the air, taking playful nips at people who were hanging out of second-floor windows. There was a huge lobster and a two-headed beast that looked something like a grotesque pig. Four or five people who looked as if they had just emerged from a pyramid towed a gigantic Egyptian lion on wheels. Abigail and Sarah and I watched the parade for a few minutes, and then found ourselves marching in it, having accepted the invitation of a friendly skeleton. We marched down the street for a block or two, in the company of witches and cowboys and cancan dancers and a ten-foot lizard. The skeleton told us that what we were marching in was the third annual Greenwich Village Halloween parade. I was furious. How could we have missed the first two?

We didn't miss any after that. We simply got our trick-or-treating done with some dispatch, even if we had to forgo a second shot at the Bubble Gum Store, and joined the parade. For several years, the Village Halloween parade seemed to me the perfect urban street event. Although the number of paraders and onlookers grew from year to year, the parade remained what one of its organizers called "a people-sized event." It remained in scale partly because it didn't have any floats. My interest in parades is usually limited by my failure to appreciate floats. I suppose I took Abigail and Sarah to the Macy's Thanksgiving Day parade now and then, but I always found my attention wandering anytime a marching band was not passing. During the Mardi Gras season in New Orleans, I have sometimes summoned up a respectful word for the floats of a prominent Carnival krewe — in the way visitors to the old Soviet Union used to inform their Intourist guides politely that the hydroelectric generating plant they had just been guided through for five hours was indeed an impressive technological accomplishment—but the sort of New Orleans Mardi Gras parade I actually look back on with nostalgia is, say, an Irish Channel marching society's street parade, consisting of a brass band of black jazz musicians, a lot of white stevedores dressed in women's clothing and the number of official beer stops that a thoughtful planner would arrange for an event that might well take place on a hot and humid day. Floats create a rigid distinction between paraders and spectators. Who can imagine stepping into the street to join, on an impulse, the Tournament of Roses parade?

In those early years, the Halloween parade was gloriously lacking in police lines and parade marshals. On the other hand, somebody had obviously done some planning of the sort designed not to call attention to itself. Somebody had arranged, for instance, for a coven of witches from PS 41 to scream and cackle and dance at Abingdon Square. Somebody had rigged the lighting that suddenly illuminated some grotesqueries on a fire escape as the parade moved down Bleecker Street. But on Halloween night, the parade just seemed to happen. Despite a larger crowd every year, there was no barrier between those watching the parade and those marching in it. For several years, it remained the sort of parade at which a garishly rouged old crone, aged ten or eleven, might suddenly leap from the sidewalk into the line of marchers to shriek at a grown-up-sized lion, who would roar back. In fact, one year, when I was particularly struck by the extent to which people played their roles in the parade—donkeys braying and witches cackling and Supermen attempting to fly through the air—I began to regret that I had chosen to wear my evil-old-man mask. It's reasonably scary-looking, I think, but it limits the wearer's capacity to act out. About the only activity consistent with the appearance of the evil-old-man is turning down a loan.

The next year — the sixth annual Greenwich Village Halloween parade — I wore my ax murderer's mask. By coincidence, everyone else in the family had decided to be a witch. Abigail and Sarah both had black capes, and Abigail, exercising the prerogative of seniority, had been given permission to wear our family's premier witch mask — a full-face rubber mask from England so terrifying that it would not have surprised me to see grown men cross themselves quickly as Abigail strolled by. She also planned to wear on her right hand a hideous rubber claw almost as scary as the mask. Alice, summoning up her full supply of enthusiasm for Halloween, had agreed to suggest a witch theme by wearing a conical witch's hat with an outfit that was otherwise, as far as I could tell, unconnected to the black arts.

I should say right away that our family happened to field three witches on the same Halloween years before anyone suggested publicly that parents who permitted their children to celebrate Halloween as small witches and ghosts and goblins and devils were putting those children in peril — softening them up for recruitment into a cult of ritualistic Satan worshippers somewhere down the road. By the middle nineties, when some concerned Christians (some of them, it turned out, the same concerned Christians who had produced a video claiming that Bill Clinton was in the habit of rubbing out his political opponents in Arkansas) began leaning on schools and churches to alter or even shut down Halloween celebrations, our girls were no longer what I believe the social service professionals call "at risk." It would be gratifying to claim that when they were children we had permitted costumes from the netherworld because we'd been able to foresee that fears about the existence of satanic cults would turn out to be overblown. (Around the time anti-Halloween protests began to turn up in the news, the first truly comprehensive nationwide investigation into satanic cults that abuse children confirmed what all previous studies had shown: there didn't actually seem to be any.) The truth, though, was that our tolerance of witch costumes was not based on an abundance of prescience but a lack of imagination. Even if we had been personally warned by Christian conservatives about the danger of satanic cults, it would have been impossible for me to look at Abigail and Sarah in their witch costumes in those days and imagine them as having started down a slippery slope that could end with them dancing around a pile of steaming rabbit innards while praying to Beelzebub. They just didn't seem the type.

Alice and Abigail and Sarah had arranged to meet me at Abingdon Square, a traditional witches' hangout, after calling on a few favorite trick-or-treat targets. I intended to watch the parade form. In those early years of the Halloween parade, it formed in the courtyard of Westbeth, a huge old telephone company building on the Hudson that had been renovated to provide apartments for people working in the arts. One of the residents of Westbeth was Ralph Lee, the creator of the huge creatures that had so astonished Abigail and Sarah and me when we first came across the parade. Lee had created the dandy for a Brecht play and the Egyptian lion for a production at Café La Mama. The Greenwich Village Halloween parade had begun, in fact, because Lee, having decided that the time had come to hold an exhibition of his creatures, simply assumed that they would be exhibited moving down the street — not a difficult thing to arrange at Westbeth, where the supply of dancers and musicians and actors and mimes and acrobats and jugglers has always exceeded the demand.

When I arrived, thirty or forty minutes before the parade was scheduled to begin, the courtyard was filled with people. A band—including a snare drummer in tails and blue sneakers, a flutist wearing a top hat and red bloomers, a pasha with a trumpet and what appeared to be a Central American terrorist on the bass drum—played constantly. Two or three people on stilts loomed over the crowd as they danced along to the music. Every few minutes, another one of Lee's creatures would emerge from the Westbeth community room—a lizard or a dragon or a monumental version of a Siamese puppet or a five-hump camel that seemed to have been fashioned from the sort of material found on sofas in old summer houses. A covey of horned and beaked creatures ran through the crowd, hooting and screaming. A gypsy dancer spun wildly to the music, taunting a man who seemed to be Mortimer Snerd. A horse warily circled a walking Statue of Liberty. The Bride of Frankenstein and five tap-dancing skeletons tapped their way across the courtyard. At one point, a huge bug seemed to cross the courtyard high in the air—pulled along on wires—and a few minutes later, with no announcement and no pushing and nobody telling anybody else where to stand, the parade started.

At Abingdon Square, our family's agreed-upon meeting place, hundreds of people were lining the curb and pressing out into the street. I couldn't spot my witches. The thought flashed across my mind, just for a moment, that they might have stopped for some early Christmas ornament shopping on Bleecker Street. I remained with the parade as it turned on Charles and headed across Seventh Avenue. On Tenth Street, the Jefferson Market Library—looking, as usual, like the city hall of a prosperous textile town in Victorian Yorkshire — had a huge spider dangling from its tallest tower. The second-floor windows were lit, and behind them an outsized version of a shadow puppet performance was being presented for the passing paraders. Not far from where I was walking, a man who was holding the frame of a television set and peering out of a hole that should have been the screen dashed back and forth among the marchers, doing advertisements for headache remedies and deodorants.

A block or so from Washington Square, I saw my witches. They came running over to report that Abigail had been one of the stars of the parade, frightening any number of fully grown cowboys and *Star Wars* characters. Alice, who finally seemed to have acquired some Halloween spirit, sounded quite enthusiastic as she recounted the greatest triumph: When Abigail frightened a boy she knew from PS 3 with her mask and horrifying cackle, the boy, apparently recognizing a familiar note in the cackle, said he would get her the next day at school. "Shake on that," Abigail had said. The boy extended his hand and then, looking down as he felt it grasp Abigail's awful claw, screamed in horror. I gazed at Abigail, who did look terrifying, even to someone who had worn the same mask himself. This time, to the extent that an ax murderer can do so, I really did beam with pride.

8

Thanksgiving Wanderings

I'm afraid it isn't possible to talk about our family's celebration of Thanksgiving without mentioning my campaign to change the national Thanksgiving dish from turkey to spaghetti carbonara. The girls had to live with that over the years. I suppose they could be compared to children who try to go about their business as if nothing is wrong even though their father is always grabbing perfect strangers by the lapels and arguing that the country is doomed if it doesn't get on the silver standard or that we all must face up to the world-domination conspiracy of the Illuminati. I didn't bother much with lapels, but I grabbed every forum I could to put forth a range of arguments, historical and practical and culinary, for abandoning turkey in favor of spaghetti carbonara. I wrote columns about how little even historians know of what was served at the first Thanksgiving meal beyond the fact that it couldn't have tasted very good, since the Pilgrims were from East Anglia, the most

English region of England—an area where to this day young women are brought up to boil the vegetables for a week and a half, in case one of the dinner guests shows up without his teeth. I wrote in books about how interesting it would be to see what those masters of the float maker's art could come up with to depict a plate of spaghetti in the Macy's Thanksgiving Day parade and how refreshing it would be to hear sports announcers call some annual tussle the Spaghetti Carbonara Day Classic. In interviews, I answered questions about whether eating spaghetti for Thanksgiving would be disrespectful to our ancestors by saying that one thing I give thanks for on Thanksgiving happens to be that those people were not *my* ancestors. For two or three years, I actually argued my case for spaghetti carbonara on the public television station in New York each November. I thought of it as an annual custom comparable to the Queen's Christmas message being broadcast every year on the BBC.

Children can be easily embarrassed by what their parents do, even if it's innocuous. When Sarah was four or five, for instance, a walk with her from the Bubble Gum Store to our house tended to inspire me to sing a couple of choruses of "The Streets of Laredo." I'm not sure why; as far as I've been able to tell, it doesn't seem to have that effect on other people. In fact, it never had that effect on me when Sarah wasn't along. Sarah claimed that she found it mortifying to walk down the street holding the hand of a grown-up who was singing "The Streets of Laredo"—particularly a grown-up who, she'd eventually have to admit under close questioning, was her father. Before we left the Bubble Gum Store, she'd sometimes turn to me and say, as if repeating a familiar but important city ordinance, "No cowboy songs on the street." I would say something like "I'm afraid I can't commit myself to a set policy at this time." For all I know, the Thanksgiving campaign was an even bigger embarrassment than cowboy songs. I wasn't privy to the playground conversations at PS 3, but I can imagine school chums saying to Abigail and Sarah, "Was that your dad on TV saying all sorts of weird stuff about eating pasta on Thanksgiving?" I don't know how they responded. Maybe, after a couple of meetings to establish a consistent policy, they'd decided that the best response was simply to mumble something noncommittal and change the subject. Maybe they said something like "He hasn't been himself lately."

When I was asked by interviewers how my own family enjoyed spaghetti carbonara on Thanksgiving, I suppose I must have done some mumbling myself. It wasn't that anybody in our family had a deep devotion to turkey that made a changeover impossible. The problem was that we were floaters on Thanksgiving. To us, Thanksgiving had always been an awkward interruption of the interlude between Halloween and Christmas—the two biggies. Almost from the first years of our marriage, we always had at least a couple of dozen people at our house for Christmas dinner. Given the proportions of the feast we put on at Christmas every year, our holding a Thanksgiving dinner at home would have been the equivalent of the Allies deciding to invade some other continent five weeks before the Normandy landings, just to keep in practice.

I think a lot of people believe that Christmas and Thanksgiving are too close together to be celebrated by similar blowouts. Why do they go along with the arrangement without complaint? Maybe they think that otherwise their neighbors will consider them un-American and tell them to go back where they came from. When Franklin D. Roosevelt tried to make Thanksgiving earlier by merely a week, the response was as if he had suggested running the stripes on the flag vertically instead of horizontally for a while. Yet Canadians, who have an international reputation for good sense, give thanks in October, which puts a little distance between the times you have to haul the extra chairs up from the basement and brace yourself for your Uncle Norton's dissertation on miles-per-gallon variations in seasonal driving conditions. No, I'm not suggesting that Americans celebrate Thanksgiving when Canadians celebrate. I happen to be on record with an explanation of why we can't have our Thanksgiving Day that much earlier: Americans all begin their Christmas shopping on the day after Thanksgiving, and if they started their Christmas shopping in the middle of October they'd run out of money sometime in November. The people who are hard to shop for wouldn't get any presents at all. That would include Uncle Norton.

Having decided early on that our family couldn't mount a traditional Thanksgiving feast that close to the Christmas extravaganza, we spent a lot of Thanksgivings at other people's houses. In the early eighties, though, I thought we had to set an example if I were to have any chance at all of getting the movement for spaghetti carbonara off the ground. Alice agreed that we'd have Thanksgiving dinner at home and would serve what I considered the authentic Thanksgiving dish. I had decided that during dinner it was only fitting for me to tell the girls my version of the story of the first Thanksgiving dinner. Yes, there is something rather silly about reading from one of your own books at the dinner table, but what are families for? At the appropriate time in the meal—I think it was just before the spaghetti carbonara was served—I picked up the book and read about some people in England called Pilgrims, "who were very strict about making sure everyone observed the Sabbath and cooked food without any flavor and that sort of thing." I told how the Pilgrims decided to go to America, where they could enjoy Freedom to Nag, and how the Indians took pity on the Pilgrims and helped them with their farming, even though the Indians thought the Pilgrims were about as much fun as teenage circumcision. "The Pilgrims were so grateful that at the end of their first year in America they invited the Indians over for a Thanksgiving meal," I read. "The Indians, having had some experience with Pilgrim cuisine during the year, took the precaution of taking along one dish of their own. They brought a dish that their ancestors had learned many generations before from none other than Christopher Columbus. Of course, the Indians didn't call him Christopher Columbus. They called him 'the big Italian fellow.' The dish was spaghetti carbonara — made with pancetta bacon and fontina and the best imported prosciutto. The Pilgrims hated it. They said it was 'heretically tasty' and 'the work of the devil' and 'the sort of thing foreigners eat.' The Indians were so disgusted that on the way back to their village after dinner one of them made a remark about the Pilgrims that was repeated down through the years and unfortunately caused confusion among historians about the first Thanksgiving meal. He said, 'What a bunch of turkeys!' "

For a number of years, simply because I'd occasionally show up on radio or television ranting about the necessity of changing the national Thanksgiving dish to spaghetti carbonara, I was perceived as anti-turkey. I did occasionally mention as opponents of my campaign "enforcers from the turkey industry," but I was not anti-turkey. As I explained to Abigail and Sarah, someone who campaigns to convince people that the economy would be better served if the country went on the silver standard is not properly described as anti-gold, even if he uses phrases like "crucified on a cross of gold" in the speeches he gives during long ascents in crowded elevators. He simply wants to put things right. In fact, fifteen years or so after I wrote the original column about a changeover to spaghetti carbonara, I developed such a strong interest in a holiday dish known as fried turkey that I went to Louisiana to learn more about it. By that time, I had realized that no real bandwagon was going to start for spaghetti carbonara, even if Alice had been willing to let our family set an example every single year. You have to be realistic about these things. Although it didn't occur to me ex-plicitly at the time, I suppose I had in the back of my mind the possibility of fashioning some compromise around fried tur-key — a dish that, from what I'd heard, could not be described, as I had often described roast turkey, as something put on earth to punish students for using the dining hall on Sunday. When I say fried turkey, I'm talking about an entire turkey being low-ered into several gallons of hot peanut oil or lard. Cautiously.

In the years since the national debate between roast turkey and spaghetti carbonara had started, an increasing number of people in southern Louisiana had turned to whole-turkey frying as a way of making a Thanksgiving bird that has crisp, golden-brown skin and white meat juicy enough to make a Pilgrim blush. The recipes for it tend to stress safety rather than tech-nique; the *Prudhomme Family Cookbook*, for instance, says, "We strongly advise you to have a complete 'dress rehearsal' . . . before you begin heating the large volume of oil." The evening before Thanksgiving, Al Dugas, a retired Baton Rouge banker I met during my research trip to Louisiana, rubs a twelve- or thirteen-pound bird with salt and cayenne pepper and then in-jects it with spices, using a syringe he bought in a veterinarians' supply store. The next morning, he heats up five or six gallons of lard in what I would call a two-missionary pot. The heat source is a portable propane cooker. It's a common enough device in southern Louisiana — the natives call it a crawfish boiler — but a visitor who sees one for the first time is tempted to inspect it for inscriptions like "Property of the National Aeronautics and Space Administration." After a turkey neck dangled in the lard has produced the satisfying crackle that indicates sufficient heat, Dugas places the turkey in a fry basket and lowers it, cautiously, into the lard. Forty-five minutes later, he withdraws it. As Grandma traditionally says at the moment she presents her Thanksgiving pumpkin pie: Voilà!

Indoor turkey frying being a serious fire hazard, Dugas does all this in the garage. Some other fried turkey chefs use carports. A garage, it turns out, is a good place for cooking. It tends to be roomier than the kitchen, lacking those little islands that people trying to help are always running into. Also, there's already a certain amount of oil on the floor. A garage tends to hold a lot of implements that catch the eye — particularly if those present don't have much to do except to watch one person watch a pot full of boiling oil for forty-five minutes. It was easy to imagine garage cooking fitting into the annual rituals of extended families that get together on Thanksgiving every year. I could picture Dad and Granddad in the garage, carrying on their annual mock argument about the relative merits of peanut oil and lard in crisping up the skin. (Dad actually believes that some health arguments could be made against using six gallons of lard; on the way home in the car every year, Granddad says to Grandma — or Stepgrandma, maybe — that peanut oil is blatantly suburban.) There's Uncle Earl piping up occasionally with some garage-inspired question like "You still use that old ten-horsepower of yours much anymore?" There's Aunt Fran coming in to help coordinate the timing of the turkey with the side dishes and saying what she says every year: "Land sakes, that hot oil scares me."

And how about the story of the first Thanksgiving? I wouldn't deny that it could be modified for fried turkey. I try to keep an open mind. The Indians show up at the Pilgrim encampment to learn that turkey is to be the main course—roast turkey, although there is no oven in evidence. "You're making a big mistake," the chief says, eyeing the huge cooking pot that the Pilgrims keep for boiling their vast and tasteless stews. This is what you might call a gourmet chief. He is the same chief who patiently demonstrated to the Pilgrims that the kernels are the only part of corn on the cob that is eaten. The Indians have brought no covered dish of their own, but they do happen to be carrying six gallons of lard, just in case. Also some spices and some large syringes. "Let me show you something," the chief says. "But first we have to have a dress rehearsal."

Even as I reworked the story of the first Thanksgiving, though, I realized that none of this would be possible for our family. When the brownstone neighborhoods of the Village were built, in the middle of the nineteenth century, nobody thought of garages. Carports hadn't even been invented. On the Upper East Side of Manhattan, I suppose, people could gather in those garages they have under luxury high-rises and lean up against their BMWs while tending a pot full of boiling lard, but it wouldn't work in our part of town. Even if I had been able to find a suitable place for lard boiling, I didn't think I could convince my family that we ought to try Thanksgiving at home again. We had gone back to floating. I can't say we were overburdened with invitations. In Alice's view, a hostess who knew she was going to be berated for having no sense of history simply because she was serving turkey instead of spaghetti carbonara might decide that, all in all, she'd rather listen to her Uncle Norton. The girls, I think, preferred to believe that the paucity of invitations had a nonideological basis — maybe something having to do with my tendency to spill cranberry sauce on my tie late in the meal.

Even when a friend did phone to invite us for Thanksgiving dinner, though, I would often say, "Thanks, but we've got plans. We're going to Chinatown." At some point in our floating, we had fallen into the custom of going to a Chinese restaurant for Thanksgiving — a Chinese restaurant that offered festive dishes, of course, like minced squab in lettuce leaves or Peking duck. To me, it seemed logical. The Thanksgiving ritual is based on eating, and, in that spirit, what I particularly wanted to give thanks for — even more fervently than for my lack of Pilgrim ancestors — was the Immigration Act of 1965. Until then, under the national quota system, this country virtually excluded Chinese while letting in as many English people as cared to come — a policy that in culinary terms bordered on the suicidal. After the immigrants who took advantage of the 1965 act began to arrive, it became increasingly safe in America to go out to dinner without carting along your own spaghetti carbonara.

Abigail and Sarah seemed delighted to fetch up in Chinatown on Thanksgiving. For one thing, I suspect they were relieved that there was no risk there of having to hear my story of the first spaghetti carbonara Thanksgiving again. When I took the time to offer appropriate holiday words during one of our Thanksgiving meals in Chinatown, I'd speak instead of what Americans should be grateful for. "If the Pilgrims had been followed to the New World by other Pilgrims," I'd say to the girls between bites of scallops with Chinese flowering chives, "we would now be eating overcooked cauliflower and warm gray meat. So count your blessings, ladies."

I was less certain about Alice's view of Thanksgiving in Chinatown. On those Chinatown Thanksgiving outings, she may have been the one person in the family lacking genuine enthusiasm. One year—I think Sarah was in high school and Abigail had come home on her Thanksgiving break from college—Alice insisted that in addition to dinner in Chinatown we all go to a Broadway musical together, "so there's something celebratory." I was baffled by that. What could be more celebratory than minced squab in lettuce leaves? And what exactly does Thanksgiving have to do with Rodgers and Hart, who would have been put in the stocks by the Pilgrims for having a sense of melody?

The issue was moot for some years, since the girls were living so far away that they sometimes didn't even get home for Halloween, let alone Thanksgiving. Then, one year, they were both able to make it back to New York for the Thanksgiving weekend. I took it for granted that we'd be eating the traditional Thanksgiving meal in Chinatown. So did they. On the phone, among the Thanksgiving customs they said they were looking forward to were salt-and-pepper shrimp and lo mein with ginger and scallion. Then, a couple of weeks before Thanksgiving, I heard Alice on the telephone with a friend of ours I'll call Nora, at whose house we'd celebrated a couple of Thanksgivings. Nora does a turkey-and-stuffing dinner that would make Norman Rockwell sorry he hadn't brought along his brushes and canvas. Alice was saying that we'd be delighted to come for Thanksgiving.

"I just love going to Nora's for Thanksgiving," she said to

me after she hung up the phone. "And so do the girls. And so do you. You know you do."

"I wonder if Nora would be willing to augment the cranberry sauce with a little take-out stuffed bean curd," I said. "Just for the sake of tradition."

9

Pet Pressure

My lizard-buying trip with the first grade from PS 3 was hardly the first time I had visited Exotic Aquatics. I had once interviewed the proprietor on the subject of geckos, small lizards that in New York have had occasional spurts in popularity because their appetite for cockroaches is said to be similar in volume to the appetite of New Yorkers for bagels and cream cheese. (Among the advantages of geckos, the proprietor of Exotic Aquatics had informed me, is that, unlike New Yorkers, they tend to be terribly shy, so that someone who has taken one on in order to do some prudent thinning of the cockroach herd is not likely to wake up and find himself eyeball to eyeball with the tiny predator.) I had also dropped in from time to time with no particular business to discuss. In those days, it was possible to while away an afternoon in Bleecker Street pet stores. You could begin with the close inspection of a sleeping snake at Exotic Aquatics and then walk up to the Abingdon Square end of the street, not far from where the coven of witches from PS 41 always stationed itself on Halloween, where there was an excellent bird store. The proprietors of the bird store had a very generous interpretation of what constituted browsing. When Sarah was going to IS 70, the romantically named intermediate school on Fifteenth Street, she passed the bird store on the walk home, and I think she stopped in most days. A couple of times, riding my bike down Bleecker Street, I glanced in and saw her with some exotic South American parrot posing on her arm. I sported neither birds nor snakes myself, but I enjoyed perusing the stock. For a few years, I suppose I deluded myself into thinking that whiling away an afternoon in Bleecker Street pet stores might be an acceptable substitute for our having a pet.

I don't mean to say that we had never harbored an animal in our house. We'd given in to requests for some smaller beasts that live in cages and, it was assumed, would not live in them for an inconvenient number of years. (You rarely hear people say, "Well, we got the kids a gerbil, and then they went off to college, and for the last ten years our lives have revolved around that gerbil.") I am now ready to acknowledge that I saw those animals basically as a way of staving off the day when we were forced to acquire a regular-sized pet whose presence we'd have to put up with for a serious chunk of time. For a while, we had a couple of long-haired guinea pigs. One day, the long-haired guinea pigs began breathing hard, and then keeled over, looking as flat as if they'd been pressed to the pavement by a steamroller. If I had put them in the girls' dollhouse, they could have been mistaken for a couple of tiny throw rugs. I diagnosed the cause of death as Totally Deflated Guinea Pig Syndrome. The deceased guinea pigs were disposed of unceremoniously, I'm sorry to say, and—let's be honest about this—perhaps illegally. We also had a rabbit for a short time. I'd rather not talk about that rabbit.

We had a lot of family discussions about the possibility of getting a larger pet of the sort that would feel free to roam around the house. (Actually, the rabbit felt free to roam around the house, which is one of the reasons I'd rather not talk about the rabbit.) I did not initiate these discussions. In fact, I tried to think of them as hypothetical, particularly after it became obvious that any purchase of a middle-sized domestic animal by our family would not involve a dog. I happen to like dogs. I suspect I had made the girls late to school more than once with tales of the dogs of my childhood—the clever Spike, for instance, whose exploits needed only slight embellishments, or the dumb and lazy pedigreed English bulldog, Sir Lancelot O'Pujilus, known as Buck, who was a sort of reverse Lassie in that he couldn't find his way home from the drugstore, a block or two away. (During my childhood in Kansas City, dogs wandered loose; I don't believe I saw a dog being walked on a leash until I visited New York as a college student.) I think I spared Abigail and Sarah the story of Chubby, the collie dog. (As it turned out, any notions that story might have put in their minds about my being, as my father would have put it, slow on the uptake were confirmed around the time they were in high school anyway: I'd just discovered, I acknowledged in print, that what Alice had been pointing out in the sky was spelled Orion rather than O'Ryan, ending years of idle curiosity on my part as to why there was one Irish constellation.) But we all felt that keeping a dog in the city would be too difficult. That left cats. When the girls were asked why we didn't have one, they always said, "Daddy hates cats," to which I always replied, "No, girls, hating cats would be prejudice, and Mommy and I have tried to bring you up to oppose prejudice wherever you encounter it. What might be fair to say is that I have never met a cat I liked."

Nobody has ever seemed satisfied with that explanation — including my daughters, who continued to say, "Daddy hates cats." I thought about some sort of compromise like "No, Daddy doesn't hate cats. Daddy hates people who go on and on about their cats." But that sounded prejudiced, too, even if I changed it to "people of any race, creed or color who go on and on about their cats." Cat owners are notoriously sensitive. Years later, I got in trouble with them for a single phrase in the introduction to a book — "When I kick at a cat, it's nearly always for good reason." They continued writing letters to upbraid me even after I offered what I thought was a satisfactory explanation for the phrase ("It was taken out of context"). When I announced my support for a plan to eradicate all of the feral cats of Australia, which are considered responsible for driving toward extinction many of the exotic marsupials that constitute part of the Australian national heritage, the complaints started all over again, even though I saw my position as less anti-cat than pro-potoroo and rufous hare-wallaby.

As Christmas approached one year, Alice and I had more or less decided, against my better judgment, to get the girls a cat. Alice's argument was that it was pathetic to see them so pet-deprived that in Nova Scotia they had taken to naming the periwinkles they collected from the rocks on one of the islands in the harbor we used for picnics. I actually didn't see anything wrong with periwinkles as pets. It seemed to me, in fact, that many of the attributes cat fanciers apply to cats — independence, the ability to care for themselves, an admirable absence of obsequiousness toward human beings—can be claimed for periwinkles as well, and in a much more manageable package. Alice said that periwinkles did not present what negotiators call a viable alternative. Finally, I agreed to a cat, although I made a last-minute effort to include the proviso that the girls would be informed that if they began talking baby talk to the cat or started talking about how marvelously aloof cats are, the cat would be sent to live with my meanest aunt. A week or so after this initial cat decision had been made, Alice and I were driving across town one evening, on the way home from having dinner with some friends. We were at Forty-third Street and Seventh Avenue. There had been silence in the car for a while. Suddenly, Alice said my name in a tone of voice that I had never heard her use before—a tone I can only call portentous. It was so portentous, in fact, that I almost stopped the car.

"What is it?" I asked.

"I have to tell you something," she said. "And I want you to try not to get excited."

I wasn't excited. I was filled with foreboding. "What is it?" I asked again.

"I think we should get the girls two cats," she said.

"Two cats!" I said. "It seems like just yesterday that all I owned was a suitcase and my typewriter. Now we're going to have two cats?"

Actually, I was relieved. I had been prepared for an announcement even more traumatic. In the movies, when a woman says her husband's name in the sort of voice Alice had used, she is usually telling him that she's leaving—departing in the morning to enter an ashram in India so she can work through her problems or running off with a fascinating pool boy who really wants to direct.

Apparently, Alice thought that the prospect of harboring two cats would be news of that magnitude for me. She had thought through the cat question, though, and she'd decided that a cat without a cat companion would get lonely. I knew better than to try to convince her that, as feline zoologists say, cats don't know from lonely. In Nova Scotia once, she'd objected to my using a bait bag in my crab traps—a bag that keeps the crabs from completely devouring the bait that had lured them into the trap. She had said that it was deceitful. I hadn't come close to convincing her that there is no such thing as being deceitful to a crab. I told Alice that it sounded as if we'd have to get two cats.

Then we ran up against what I think of as the maven problem. A maven is someone who is knowledgeable in some particular field, but, more than that, he's the person you depend on for guidance in that field. In New York, everybody's got a maven for everything. Standing at an intersection or riding the subway, you hear people saying, "My computer maven says this is not the time to buy a laptop" or "I thought I could breathe a little better, but my allergy maven tells me that drug they gave me is considered a thing of the past." Even though a good maven may know where bargains are to be found, having a maven may drive up the cost. Being a specialist in the field, the maven is likely to have high standards. If you want to buy a start-out piano for your kids in New York, the maven you consult may have come to the city from Iowa with dreams of being a concert pianist. He'll tell you that if you absolutely must get an upright, you have to get a thirty-five-inch Steinway; buying anything else for the kids to play chopsticks on is at least a waste of money and probably a scandal. Our cat maven said that what we wanted was not a couple of kittens from the animal shelter but two Siamese.

Siamese cats, as it turns out, are noted for their yowling. That's not the sort of thing that would trouble a cat maven; in fact, she might, I suppose, welcome the yowling as an indication that the cats in question were authentic full-breed Siamese. The two Siamese kittens we got were brothers. Abigail and Sarah, using *Anna and the King of Siam* as a research tool, gave them Siamese names—Tuptin and Mao. I decided to refer to them as Maish and Benny, in honor of two of my uncles. In practice, nobody called them anything except "the cats." They were impossible to tell apart—or to tell from any other Siamese cat, for that matter. Even their yowls were identical. Alice thought one of them was friendlier than the other, but I offered the possibility that each of them was a bit friendlier than usual part of the time. After we'd had them for a while, I could still state that I had never met a cat I liked. These cats spent their time creeping around the house, occasionally letting loose with a terrible yowl. Occasionally, as a change of pace from yowling, they threw up. Or maybe only one of them threw up; there was no way to know. When they wanted to give themselves a special treat, they searched out something in the house one of us particularly valued—a favorite sweater, a small piece of folk art— and destroyed it. As my father would have said, what's to like?

After what seemed like decades, one of the cats got sick and died a lingering, hideously expensive death. The financial burden of this cat's final weeks on earth could be used to argue for a single-payer national health insurance system for cats. To this day, I can be going about my daily tasks with good cheer when a stricken look suddenly comes over my face. I have just thought of what my father would have said if he had known how much I spent on the final illness of a cat I didn't like and couldn't even distinguish from another cat I didn't like.

The girls were off to college by then, and we decided that something had to be done about what we could only call the remaining cat, since nobody had the foggiest idea which one it was. Alice thought it might be a good idea to give the remaining cat to someone who would give it a good home, perhaps with other cats. "I think he's lonely here without his brother," she said.

"Absolutely," I said. "I couldn't agree with you more."

10

Entertaining Possibilities

M aybe I wasn't being absolutely forthcoming when I said that zipping and unzipping snowsuit zippers (or was it trying to fasten diaper pins?) was the only aspect of having children around the house that I was happy to be rid of. When you no longer have children at home, you're liberated from having to become deeply involved in certain issues—for instance, the long public discussion, held after our daughters were grown, about whether the amount of trash that children watch on television could be limited effectively by some sort of technofix like the V-chip. I did notice that nobody in the discussion demonstrated much interest in the fact that in most American households the only people who understand how to use such electronic devices as V-chips are the children. Around the time the V-chip began to be talked about, I'd written a story about a couple I called Bennett and Linda Weber. The Webers thought they were pleased that their twenty-six-year-old son, Jeffrey, had finally decided to move out of the house — Linda Weber said that if Jeffrey was ever going to find himself, something he talked about a lot, he probably should look someplace other than his own room — but when he left they realized they had lost their ability to tape. Their fancy VCR was the equivalent of a BMW in the garage of someone who didn't know how to drive. Their even fancier stereo system was the Jaguar parked next to the BMW. As the V-chip discussion went on, I could envision a younger version of Bennett Weber trying to block, say, programs that contained strong language and instead doing something that caused the set to transmit nothing but cooking shows. "Do something!" he says, turning to the child he's trying to protect from horrible television programming. That child is Jeffrey, at fourteen, who says with a grin, "Don't worry, Pop. I'll take care of it." Once again, the inmates are in charge of the asylum.

The V-chip discussion reminded me that in deciding how to control what our children watched on television when they were growing up, we somehow took as our authority not Benjamin Spock but Benito Mussolini. Abigail and Sarah were only allowed to watch certain programs, and we usually watched the programs with them. There weren't many. *Sesame Street*, which came along around the same time Abigail did, was one of them, I'm happy to say; I attribute my ability to do a widely praised Cookie Monster imitation to the hours I spent in front of the set in those early days of *Sesame Street*'s run. A little later, one of the other approved programs, for reasons I can't remember, was *Little House on the Prairie*, which I found approximately as interesting as the Troop Information and Education lectures I was made to attend in the Army. I don't believe any sitcoms escaped our family equivalent of the Vatican Index. To watch a sitcom, the girls would have had to concoct a reason to visit a neighbor's house, like secret opponents of some Eastern European Communist regime sneaking off to listen to the Voice of America on the radio of someone who had somehow managed to overcome the regime's jamming efforts.

Looking back on that era, our television policy sounds so uncharacteristically strict that it's hard to believe that I'm remembering accurately. If we were lenient on small matters and strict on large ones, did that mean that Alice and I considered television a large matter? That doesn't seem possible. I've been assured by my daughters, though, that when it came to what could be watched on the tube, rigid and arbitrary and oppressive fiats were definitely in place. Abigail, in fact, maintains that such rules were not completely uncharacteristic.

"I consider junk food in the same category," she has said to me.

"Junk food?"

"Yes, junk food. Did you ever get suspicious about why we had so many sleepovers next door at Tamar and Ariela's on Saturday night? Twinkies and *The Love Boat*."

According to Abigail's recollection, in about third grade—at a time, I should say, when her eye for injustice was already so sharp that she was referred to as the Amnesty International representative at our house—she pointed out to us that after her bedtime a school friend of hers got to stay up to watch both *Happy Days* and *Laverne & Shirley*.

"I don't see anything unfair about that," I said, when she told me about it many years later. "If you'd been awake, you wouldn't have been allowed to see them anyway."

Sarah says that living under the rules of strict censorship in her own home was probably what whetted her appetite for the sort of programming she was denied; as an adult, she is, in effect, our sitcom maven, as well as our movie maven and our final authority on what is cool and what is not cool. Sarah's interest in sitcoms might be compelling evidence that bans on television watching are counterproductive, except that Abigail, growing up under the same deprivation, doesn't seem to have much interest in sitcoms. I am sometimes tempted to defend our policy with the detached view of the situation that you often hear from self-protective politicians in Washington: whatever mind-rotting occurred did not occur on my watch.

Given the fact that I had gone off watch long before the debate about the V-chip got cranked up, I hardly paid any attention to it until a friend of ours named Molly, who was then eleven, confessed to her parents that she had been watching Martha Stewart on television. Picture this: Molly's parents are off at their respective offices, under the assumption that their daughter is doing her homework or at least taking in something broadening on the history channel. Molly, meanwhile, is planted in front of the tube while Martha Stewart demonstrates how the fall foliage in your backyard can, with a little imagination, be transformed into the perfect centerpiece for that festive Sunday brunch. I don't know if Molly's confession to her parents included handing over something like an exquisite Christmas wreath or the ultimate baked apple. The details have never come out.

Molly's parents did not panic. They are pretty cool, even by Molly's standards. Not long after this happened, we all discussed it over Sunday supper at a homey New Jersey restaurant called The Cafe — in Rosemont, not far from where Molly and her parents live — and voices were not raised. The conversation was so lacking in tension, in fact, that I felt it might be all right to ask Molly what she thought of Martha Stewart.

"She seems to have a lot of time on her hands," Molly said.

That remark indicated to me that Molly had almost certainly come away from the experience unscathed. A little later in the meal, though, it was revealed that the same could not be said for her experience with the television advertising campaign against drug use—just the sort of programming that most parents hope their children will watch attentively. This came out while we were discussing The Cafe's profound understanding of breakfast. I had introduced that subject after Molly was kind enough to allow me a taste of what she'd ordered as a main course—a dish that I would associate with breakfast but is carried on the menu throughout the day as "Potatoes from Heaven." When somebody said that the chef did have a great touch with omelettes, Molly made the sort of face I became familiar with when our own children were around her age and someone at the dinner table carried on about some blissful experience with a wild mushroom or a raw oyster.

Why did Molly grimace at the thought of eating eggs? Because several years before, she'd seen the most famous and widely praised drug commercial in the anti-drug campaign. The commercial opens with a shot of a raw egg, while a voice says, "This is your brain." The egg is then dumped onto a sizzling griddle while the voice says, "This is your brain on drugs." The commercial may well have put a number of teenagers off drugs. It put at least one six-year-old in New Jersey off eggs.

But, you might be thinking, the commercial still did some good for Molly by blunting her interest in eggs: at age eleven, she must have had the lowest cholesterol count in the entire sixth grade. I wouldn't know about that. One of the many pleasant characteristics of my conversations with Molly over the years is that she never talks about cholesterol. No, the lesson I would draw from Molly's problem with eggs is that old one about the doctrine of unintended consequences. It's the lesson that was always drawn from the Soviet propaganda film of Cold War legend that had been intended to demonstrate the brutality of strike-busting thugs beating peaceful workers in Detroit but apparently left Russian audiences impressed instead with the fact that all the workers seemed to be wearing decent shoes. Even adults can come away with the wrong message — like the garment manufacturer who, according to the old story, remarked while walking from the theater after the opening night of *Death of a Salesman*, "That New England territory never was any good." The vulnerability of children to the doctrine of unintended consequences is, I suppose, an argument for watching whatever they watch with them.

That was fine when what we were watching was *Sesame Street*. Something like *Little House on the Prairie* made it more of a strain, although I found that I could liven things up a bit by occasionally taking the side of that storekeeper's wife who was always being mean to Laura ("You've got to admit that kid could get on your nerves"). I think I came close to drawing the line at children's theater. We had assumed children's theater would be terrific in New York. The city is, of course, full of aspiring actors who have to put in a certain number of years before becoming toasts of Broadway; they'll appear in just about any sort of theater in the meantime, while supporting themselves as waitresses or copy-shop clerks or handymen. They form sort of an underground economy, like undocumented aliens in Southwestern cities. I once wrote about a neighbor of ours who, in interviewing prospective waiters for a bar he was opening, found that so many of them were aspiring actors that he finally said, "This isn't a play about a bar. It's a bar."

When Abigail and Sarah were small, there were, in fact, a couple of inspired troupes of children's entertainers in New York—the Paper Bag Players, for instance, and Bil Baird's puppet theater. On the whole, though, children's theater in New York made me wonder how much worse tired sitcoms and Saturday morning cartoons could be. In performance after performance, children would shrink into the corner of their seats as the foolishly dressed people onstage favored them with stupid pratfalls or double entendres that would make any grown-up groan. I finally concluded that children's theater troupes are formed in New York by having someone go around the city for months looking for the loudest person at every party—the one with the crudest jokes and the most shameless mugging and the most embarrassing clothing. "You are a natural for the Hunky Dunky Players," the scout says to the loudmouth. "Oh, gee golly whiz!" the loudmouth says loudly. And off they go to rehearse a burlesque version of *Jack and the Beanstalk*.

When Abigail was around six and Sarah was around three, the standards of our theatergoing with the girls took an abrupt change for the better. We got a telephone call from some friends of ours who ran a jazz hall in New Orleans. They were in New York on tour with one of their bands. They had two boys, of about the age of our girls, who had been taken along on the bus with the band from infancy. The boys were accustomed to the varying bedtimes and accommodations and meals found on the road, although apparently one of the first sentences one of them uttered had been in some Midwestern motel dining room while eating rice—rice that, unlike the rice he had been fortunate enough to eat in French Quarter joints like Buster Holmes's Red Beans and Rice Restaurant all his short life, was not roughly eighty-proof garlic. "Mommy," he said, "the rice tastes funny."

The phone call was an invitation for the entire family to go to a Broadway show that night—a musical called *Pippin*, about the son of Charlemagne. "Meet us at the theater a few minutes before eight," our friend said. "We've already got the tickets."

"I don't think Sarah has ever been up that late," I said. "She's known among the Broadway crowd for conking out just before curtain time."

"So give her a nap."

That was not out of the question. It was Abigail who'd been so reluctant to have a snooze in the daytime at that age that I started explaining to people that she refused to take a nap until American troops left Southeast Asia. We managed to get Sarah to take a nap.

I think if I'd had to review *Pippin* in a few words I would have said, "Very little, brilliantly presented." There was more going on—more dancing and singing and juggling and tumbling—than in a year of children's theater. All of it was done gracefully. Nobody mugged. Nobody told dreadfully corny jokes and then waited for the audience to respond. Sarah adored it. She stayed awake for the entire play, most of the time with her mouth open in astonishment. Abigail adored it, too. That evening marked our liberation from the theater troupes composed of the loudest person at every party. From then on, we went to musicals—not to Broadway musicals, except on special occasions such as birthdays and at least one Thanksgiving. We went to the musicals that are constantly being held in Manhattan in places like church halls and neighborhood playhouses. The quality of the productions was remarkably high. A lot of the people we saw seemed ready for Broadway to me, whether they were still waiting tables or not. In places like the Equity Library Theater and St. Bart's Community Hall, we saw *Guys and Dolls* and *Anything Goes* and *Allegro* and *Carousel* and *Kiss Me, Kate* and *West Side Story* and *The Pajama Game.*

Was there a hidden agenda here? In the back of our minds did we have some educational program worthy of reporting to the inspector from the Responsible Parenting League? *Kiss Me, Kate* and *West Side Story* are, after all, based on Shakespeare plays. A number of the musicals we saw—*Paint Your Wagon*, for instance, and *South Pacific*—are about distinctive periods in American history. I suppose it's possible to conjure up a scene that takes place in, say, intermediate school American history. The class has reached the period of Western expansion. (It's already the beginning of May, so it appears that anything that happened from the time of World War II onward will have to be skipped again this year.) "Does anyone here know anything about the way land was acquired by settlers in the state of Oklahoma?" the teacher, Ms. Witherspoon, asks. There is silence in the room. "Anybody?" Ms. Witherspoon repeats. Finally, from the back row, a single hand goes up. It's the little Trillin girl, the same girl who earlier in the year, during a social studies unit on the American labor movement, gave such a clear explanation of the place of hourly wages in collective bargaining by using a pajama factory strike as an example ("Seven and a half cents doesn't mean a hell of a lot," she'd said. "Seven and a half cents doesn't mean a thing. But give it to me every hour, forty hours every week . . ."). Standing at her desk now, the little Trillin girl presents a lucid capsule history of the Oklahoma land rush and the various forces in the territory at the time. She ends by offering to sing one of Curley's big Act Two numbers. Ms. Witherspoon is confirmed in her earlier impression that the little Trillin girl is a genius.

I can't say that I ever had that fantasy, but I'll acknowledge that the girls' growing interest in musicals planted another thought in my head which could qualify as, if not a hidden agenda, at least a quiet little side benefit. From time to time, I wondered if the music of people like Cole Porter and Frank Loesser and Stephen Sondheim might provide at least a temporary inoculation against the sort of rock music that, played at its customary volume, tends to bring calls of distress from the neighbors. I don't mean that I was among those who thought that the rock beat infected children in a way that tended to turn their hair orange and compel them to sass their elders. It never occurred to me that the warnings about American children being corrupted by the lyrics of popular songs should be taken seriously, and I eventually read the results of a study in California showing that most teenagers do not pay any attention to the lyrics of songs, even on those rare occasions when the lyrics are actually intelligible. It wasn't that I thought rock music wicked or harmful. As a parent who happens to like Cole Porter songs himself, I was just indulging myself in a selfish little daydream.

For a while, they did seem inoculated. Abigail must have been the only ten-year-old in the neighborhood with a picture of Richard Rodgers on her bulletin board. When one of the girls had a birthday, part of the celebration was often an early-evening appearance at Windows on the World, on top of the World Trade Center—not the main restaurant but the bar area then known, alas, as the Hors d'Oeuvrerie. The girls were fond of both the view and the chocolate cake. Alice would have tea. I had a scotch. There was a piano in the area, played by one of those New York cocktail pianists of indeterminate age who, seemingly without effort, could play what are sometimes called the Standards as long as anyone remained to listen. On a couple of those birthdays, Abigail and Sarah left the table to make a request, and I could see the pianist's face tighten as they approached. He figured, I suspect, that he was about to be asked to play some song whose very name made him shudder. The girls would say something like "Do you know anything from *Kiss Me, Kate?*" The pianist's face would brighten in surprise and delight, as if it were his birthday being celebrated.

Sooner or later, of course, the musical theater vaccine lost its punch. Our Off-Off-Broadway theatergoing was hardly the girls' only access to music. They naturally developed an interest in the same sort of songs their friends were listening to. They were patient in trying to answer our occasional questions about why some singer whose name we had just heard seemed to be so famous or how some group whose music we were listening to in the car achieved the intended effect ("Is that guy singing, or what?"). Eventually, the girls attempted to give their parents a capsule education in contemporary music. On Christmas, they would often give us a tape or a CD. "It's part of your course," they'd explain. If it had appeared in a course catalogue, our course might have been described as "Music Appreciation 201: A survey of contemporary sound, not including the extremes. Starting gently with Simon and Garfunkel, for the benefit of students born before World War II, the syllabus moves gradually to the Indigo Girls and, for those who are able to continue, on to the study of the sort of rock that has apparently in the past made some parents say 'guts and throwup.' " Looking back, it seems remarkable how quickly we passed from the time when we were advising them what to watch to the time when they were advising us what to listen to.

11

Sticking to It

October after October, "What are you going as?" remained a question asked constantly around our house. In a column I was doing for *The Nation* during part of the girls' childhood, I sometimes mentioned costume ideas suggested by people outside our family—particularly a mythic colleague I called Harold the Committed, who thought that our Halloween parade costumes, like just about everything else in our lives, reflected insufficient political commitment. *The Nation* has long been a redoubt of the left—when more conservative people asked why I wrote for it I always said that it was the closest magazine to my house—and Hal the C, as I referred to him in less formal moments, was the spokesman for the *Nation* loyalists who suspected that I might have let the agony of the Scottsboro Boys slip from my memory. One year, I reported that he wanted Abigail to go to the parade as Emma Goldman. Abigail went that year as a box of M&M's. When he suggested that Sarah go as "the dangers posed to our society by the military-industrial complex," I replied, "Harold, I don't think we have anybody at home who can sew that well." Sarah went that year as a chocolate-chocolate-chip ice-cream cone with chocolate sprinkles.

Yes, a food theme seemed to run through the girls' costumes. One year, Sarah went as a jar of Hellman's mayonnaise. When Sarah was about nine, a babysitter, through judicious use of crepe paper and foam rubber, actually managed to transform her into a bacon, lettuce and tomato sandwich. My own costume tastes were even more narrowly focused. Not that I didn't start out every year with a completely open mind and a commitment to freeing myself from what seemed to have become a costume rut. Somehow, though, I always went back to my ax murderer's mask. I'd purchased it in London. One afternoon, strolling past a row of shops near Charing Cross Road, I came upon a mask store. In the window was a truly hideous mask—a rubber mask that covered the entire face, except for two holes that permitted the wearer's own eyes to become part of the effect. Its gnarled features—particularly a great lump of a nose—suggested the rather slow wood-gatherer in a Gothic movie who doesn't say much until some perceived slight puts him over the edge at a moment when he happens to be carrying his ax. I wanted the mask instantly. I realized that I had always wanted a mask like that. It occurred to me that I could rationalize buying the mask by its obvious utility in the movies we were beginning to make with the girls in the summertime. Then it occurred to me that I was a grown-up, which meant that if I saw something I'd always wanted—at least something I'd always wanted that cost only five or ten pounds—I could simply buy it. You might say, in other words, that I imported that ax murderer's mask.

As Halloween approached every year, I'd think of going as something new, but then I'd pull out the ax murderer's mask and be swept away by its essential rightness. For some years, I contented myself with making changes and additions in the accessories, like a Shakespearean actor who has played Hamlet in countless productions but somehow manages to add a few new expressions or mannerisms every time he does the part. In a newspaper column one year—a column in which I acknowledged that I sometimes began talking about my Halloween costume at some length with Alice while we were sitting on the dock in Nova Scotia in August, even though she rarely replied—I described my costume as it had developed up to the previous year's parade: "The previous Halloween, I'd worn my ax murderer's mask, a baseball hat that had on the front the name 'South Brooklyn Casket Company' and a picture of a casket, an old bathrobe and, fastened to my forearm, an extremely realistic rubber lizard. I'd been wearing the baseball hat for a couple of years—it was a gift from my friend Fred, who moved from New York to Maryland, where he didn't think he'd be needing it—and I'd always worn the lizard. But the bathrobe was a new touch."

In the early years, we developed our own way of participating in the parade. We'd get to Westbeth early to watch the formation—the courtyard reminded Abigail and Sarah of a gypsy encampment—and then we'd try to find a place toward the head of the line of march. When the parade turned from Bleecker onto Charles Street, we'd stop to sit on the front stoop of some friends of ours and watch the paraders who had been behind us. Charles Street is narrow enough to afford a good view, and for a year or two there was a bonus in a large open window across the way: speakers blared out "Don't Cry for Me, Argentina" from *Evita* while dead ringers for Juan and Eva

Perón waved to the crowd below. One year, we asked some friends we'd run into if they'd like to stop back at our house after the parade, and after that our Halloween ritual was always capped off with a party.

The party developed traditions of its own. Around the time of the fifth or sixth annual Greenwich Village Halloween parade, I had published a story about four young women we'd run across while they were working as street entertainers on Sheridan Square. Their group was called the Steinettes. It had been formed originally to provide some time frames for the one-man show that a comic named Phil Stein performed at Westbeth and called "The Phil Stein Show, starring Phil Stein and Featuring the Steinettes." My story was called "Discovering the Steinettes," because it turned out that the Steinettes, who had an absolutely terrific act, were discovered almost weekly. They kept being discovered in just the way all the actors we saw in children's theater and Off-Off-Broadway musicals dreamed of being discovered — by some producer or director or agent or promoter — but being discovered turned out to have very little effect on their lives or their fortunes. The Steinettes had become friends of the family, and they customarily showed up at the Halloween party to entertain with a few a cappella doo-wop numbers — a performance that almost invariably caused some deeply impressed guest to discover them all over again.

Through a friend I'd met on another story — Tom Chaney, of Horse Cave, Kentucky — we arranged one year to acquire a country ham from a noted Horse Cave purveyor named J. T. Mitchum. The Mitchum country ham also became a custom, enhanced for several years in a row by Tom himself arriving from Philadelphia, where he had lighted temporarily in one of his non–Horse Cave periods, to cook it according to the ancient and foolproof Chaney family recipe. At first, I kept the ham on top of a filing cabinet in my office until Halloween arrived. Once we got the marauding Siamese cats, I got into the habit of hanging it from a beam between two posts in the living room; I figured that they couldn't get up there to eat it and it was too high to throw up on. One year, a number of people we didn't know were coming over in the week before Halloween—our house was the setting for a fund-raising party for some arts project—and Alice thought some of the guests might be taken aback by the sight of the ham, which, as befitted its authenticity, was horribly ugly and still bore signs of having been wrapped in the *Hart County News*. I solved the problem by posting a three-by-five card, of the sort used in art galleries, on one of the posts next to the ham. It said, " 'Country Ham,' by J. T. Mitchum. Meat and wire composition."

As our family traditions surrounding the Halloween parade settled into place, the parade itself changed. From the start, I'd found that my delight at having discovered the parade was tempered by doubt that it could survive for long. Events of unstructured enjoyment in American cities tend to have limited life spans; at some point, they are almost always crushed or transmogrified by the sheer weight of attendance. Ralph Lee had hoped that the people who came from outside the Village to see the parade would be inspired to start similar events in their own neighborhoods, but it didn't work out that way. They simply returned the next year and brought their friends. From year to year, Abigail and Sarah and I and the other paraders had increasing difficulty making our way through crowds that had spilled out into the street. At some point, police barricades became necessary. Then it was decided that the narrow Village streets of the original parade route were unsafe for such a large crowd. The parade was rerouted straight up Sixth Avenue. There were thousands of spectators and battalions of police. There were floats—not the sort of floats you'd see in the Rose Bowl, it's true, but still floats. Ralph Lee and his creatures dropped out. I didn't blame him. The parade had become a different event, no longer what he'd had in mind.

We stayed in. We had loved the old parade, but what we'd loved more, I realize now, was having what had become an annual family ritual in late October—deciding on costumes, making our way across the Village to get into the line of march, comparing notes at the party afterwards about the astonishing characters we'd seen. Until Abigail and Sarah came along, I'd never fully understood how children cling to family rituals. I suppose it comes from the same instincts that make them wary of change—changing schools, say, or houses: "They're loath to surrender the familiar," I wrote in *Messages from My Father*, in discussing the resistance children have to change. "They have no reason to believe that what they have—what they're reasonably sure they have a firm grasp on—can be replaced."

Our kids liked doing the same thing every year, or even every few weeks. Every year, we went to the same place to sing carols on Christmas Eve. Every year we had a large crowd of people— at its core, the same people who had always come—to our house on Christmas Day. Every year we had an Easter egg hunt in the courtyard next to our house. Regularly, the girls and I went to the Lower East Side or to Chinatown. Regularly, we all went to Goldberg's Pizzeria on Sunday evening so that Abigail and Sarah, with Fats Goldberg looking over their shoulders, could construct their own pizzas. When Sarah or Abigail had a birthday party, Fats always showed up bearing a heart-shaped pizza, with the birthday girl's initials done in green peppers. Every summer when school was out—or, I have to admit, a couple of times when we'd decided that by all rights it should be out—we left for Nova Scotia. Every year we made the same stops coming back from Nova Scotia. Every year, we marched in the Halloween parade. After the parade changed enough to be almost unrecognizable, we still marched in the Halloween parade.

I still wore my ax murderer's mask, with appropriate accessories. We were separated from the spectators by police barricades, of course, but now and then I'd manage to startle someone by sticking my hand across the barrier, almost as if to shake hands, until the lizard on my arm was virtually in the victim's face—a variation on the move Abigail had made with her hideous claw in an early parade to scare that kid she knew from school. We tried not to go on about the good old days. Occasionally, we even found some way in which the new parade was an improvement—more room on Sixth Avenue for group costumes, for instance, which made it possible one year for forty teachers to show up as Imelda Marcos's shoes. When Abigail and then Sarah got to high school, we continued to march up Sixth Avenue, often accompanied by their school friends. In fact, we didn't stop after they went off to college. They were close enough to New York to come home for the major holidays.

The year they were both in college at the same time—the year that would be known in the Chinese calendar as the Year of the Tuition—Sarah showed up with a half dozen outriders. They had decided to go to the parade as the game show *Wheel of Fortune*. I was pleased to see them putting together a group costume of such ambition, although I had also been impressed the year before when Sarah, after sprucing up the slightly wilted lettuce with fresh green crepe paper, had marched in the parade again in the BLT costume she'd worn when she was nine. From what I could gather about what Abigail was up to as she rummaged through the costume bag, she was planning to go as the cultural elite or Saddam Hussein's cabinet, whichever one turned out to be easier to put together. Alice was wearing her usual chic outfit, mildly accessorized for the occasion by a twenties hat and a feather boa. That day, though, I'd given her a present that added an entirely new element to the ensemble — an orange-and-black necklace made out of replicas of candy corn and goblin faces that blinked on and off. It had set me back $7.95, I told Alice, but I think an unexpected gift of jewelry now and then is the sort of thing that keeps a marriage vibrant.

When everyone else was pretty much costumed, I was still rummaging through the costume bag. "I want you to see me break out of my ax murderer's rut," I said to my daughters.

"Maybe next year," Abigail said.

"Next year?" I said hopefully.

"Don't worry, Daddy," Sarah said. "We'll be back next year."

But there came a year, of course, when they weren't back. They were both living in California. I can't say that I'd never realized that this could happen. At some point I acknowledged in print that when our daughters were about two and five I'd decided that they were at the perfect age and had begun having fantasies about some sort of freezing process that might keep them there. There was no such freezing process on the market. Assuming, in the traditional American way, that the technology would come along by and by, I renewed my fantasies several times during the time they were growing up—they always seemed to be at the perfect age — but the freezing process never surfaced. Meanwhile, they started getting older at what seemed to me a constantly accelerating rate. Pretty soon, they were so old that they both lived three thousand miles away from their own costume bag. There came a year when someone I knew asked me whatever happened to the Halloween party we used to have at our house — he might have been wondering whether he had simply been cut off the list for some offense like unpersuasive costuming — and I said, "We ran out of kids." At one point in that period, I wrote a piece about Halloween that included a description of how quiet the night of October 31 had become for a onetime reveler I called Horace:

"When Horace's kids were small, he's told me, he loved taking them around the neighborhood to trick-or-treat. He enjoyed the opportunity to have a little chat with neighbors he sometimes didn't see from year to year. It was always fun to see what each child had chosen as a costume — a witch, a Mars bar, Big Bird — and, Horace admitted to me, he rather liked getting into his own costume. He was a pirate captain. He approached each house shouting 'Avast, ye hearties!' If his gang ran across people who offered apples or granola or whole-grain sugarless biscuits or anything other than the disgusting teeth-rotters that Horace thought proper for Halloween, he threatened to run them through.

"All that is over now. On October 31, Horace and his wife sit home, recalling ghosts of Halloweens past. Even the occasional visit of trick-or-treaters doesn't do much to cheer them up. Horace likes to see the neighborhood kids in their Halloween costumes, but he finds himself so envious of the accompanying adults that it's difficult to muster much cheerfulness.

"A year ago, his wife persuaded him that he might feel better if he wore his old pirate captain costume when he opened the door to trick-or-treaters, but a little boy in the first group of callers—a four-year-old who was ferociously costumed as a snaggle-toothed monster—burst into tears at the sight of him. Now Horace wears his cardigan—which he was hoping would make him feel like Mister Rogers but somehow makes him feel more like Mr. Wilson, the grump who lives next door to Dennis the Menace.

"Horace and I agree about what's causing the problem for both of us and a lot of our contemporaries. Not long after you run out of your own kids to take trick-or-treating—or to take to the zoo or the ball game or fishing—you're supposed to have grandchildren to take their place. There are no grandchildren in sight. When you read about the effects of changing marriage and childbearing patterns in this country—women waiting until after their career has taken hold before they get married, for instance, or couples living together for years before making it official and having a couple of kids—what you don't read about is that this is causing what can only be called a grandchildren gap.

"This is why Horace spent this past Halloween at home in his cardigan, feeling like Mr. Wilson. He understands that. He understands that twenty years ago someone the age of his youngest daughter would have probably been the mother of two rather than an assistant district attorney. Horace wants his daughter to do whatever makes her happy. He's proud of her. He has every reason to believe that she is a terrific assistant district attorney. On the other hand, he misses his pirate captain costume."

Was I Horace in the story as well as myself? Well, for one thing, I was not sitting home on Halloween, dressed in some ratty cardigan. At about six-thirty on that Halloween evening, I would take off my ratty cardigan, put on my ax murderer's mask, complete with accessories, and join the Halloween parade for the march up Sixth Avenue. Fathers cling to family rituals, too.

"Oh, Daddy's fine," Alice had said earlier in the day, when Abigail phoned from California to see how her father was taking his abandonment as the big night approached. "Archibald is coming over to march in the parade with him."

Archibald, an animated little boy who was three or four at the time, is the son of a friend who had moved just around the corner from us. That year, he was impressive as the Lion King, from the Disney movie. The next year, he was a skeleton. By then it seemed clear that our marching in the Halloween parade together every year had become a sort of ritual.

12

Nuptials du Jour

In the middle eighties, Alice and I attended a lovely wedding
ceremony in Central Park, in a rose garden whose existence
I hadn't even been aware of. It was a simple ceremony,
attended by a small crowd—just families and a few friends and
the bride and groom and their two-year-old daughter. As the
ceremony went on, the bride and groom's daughter, who was
standing next to them, got a bit cranky, and the brother of the
groom shouted out from the crowd, "You should have waited
until she was a little older."

Even before that experience, I was aware, of course, that
wedding ceremonies had changed a lot since Alice and I got
married in 1965—during a period that I usually describe as
being, in terms of the history of marital relations, in that awkward period between dowries and prenuptial agreements. The
year of our marriage was actually a couple of years before what
people refer to as The Sixties began in earnest. What you were

likely to see at a wedding in 1965 was still pretty predictable: a bride and a groom, with their children still in the future; a licensed member of the clergy or the judiciary to officiate; rather formal clothing for both the wedding party and the guests. In fact, Alice and I were thought of as mildly eccentric for getting married in London, in a registry office. We thought of it as simply our twist on the old New York custom of popping down to City Hall and having a clerk there officiate over what Fats Goldberg always refers to as "closing the deal." Alice wanted to avoid putting a burden on her parents, who were what the English would have called poorly, and my parents had assured us that getting married in London was all right with them as long as we promised to come to Kansas City at our first opportunity so that they could invite friends and relatives to the sort of reception we thought we were managing to avoid by being in England.

We had a brief ceremony at Caxton Hall, Westminster, witnessed by a couple of good friends. It was Friday the 13th, because that happened to be the first day we could be married after fulfilling the residency requirement. The ceremony was presided over by a marriage registrar who saved me the trouble of having to make up a suitable name for him in the stories I'd tell about the ceremony; he had already been christened Barry J. Digweed. After he had pronounced us man and wife, Barry J. Digweed informed us that one of the afternoon papers had phoned the previous day to ask if he would, by chance, be presiding on Friday the 13th at a wedding ceremony that included an attractive young bride. He wanted to warn us that there might be a photographer outside. He said he hoped we didn't mind. I assumed that Barry J. Digweed, wittingly or unwittingly, was playing a role in some sort of prank organized by some newspaper people I knew in London. My plan was to emerge from Caxton Hall Registry Office, with my new bride on my arm, hold my hands up in front of our faces, in the time-honored response to intruding paparazzi, and say, "We're just friends." But when we came out of the building the photographer who greeted us was so palpably authentic that I totally forgot my plan. The line vanished from my mind. The photographer took his picture of us walking hand in hand down the sidewalk in front of Caxton Hall. As I thought back on the incident the next day, it occurred to me that I hadn't minded having our wedding on Friday the 13th but I did wonder whether a muffed line was a promising way to begin a marriage.

Although it may not have been apparent in 1965, the wedding conventions taken for granted by the fifties guys were beginning to fray. Within a few years, it wouldn't have surprised anyone to see the bride and groom standing in a field of daisies, nodding along to the appropriate passage of Tibetan poetry and Australian Aboriginal didjeridoo music before exchanging promises to respect each other's space. The American wedding was out of the box. Anything was on. That was one reason I was surprised years later when Ross Perot announced that he was dropping out of the 1992 presidential campaign partly because a Republican dirty-tricks squad had plans to disrupt his daughter's wedding. Wedding disruption as a political dirty trick was as new to me as to anyone else, but I had another question about a wedding in America in 1992 being disrupted: How would you tell? For people whose notions of proper ceremonies were formed before the cultural sea change of the late sixties and early seventies—a category that must have included a large part of the guests at the Perot nuptials in Dallas—a lot of weddings looked disrupted already.

How would anybody know whether some unusual wrinkle came about because of Republican dirty tricks or the cultural liberation of the betrothed? Sure, tricksters could slip into the organist's loft the evening before and replace the Bach sheet music with the latest outrage from Run DMC. But the guests might simply assume that the happy couple — considerably cooler than the previous generation, at least on the Perot side — had requested such music. These days, if the traditional ministerial request for any objections to the union were answered by a well-dressed Young Republican rising to announce, "I have here in my hand a lewd computer-generated picture of the bride," the minister might say, "Why don't you pass it around." Even the bride might say, "Why don't you pass it around." In these matters, we've gone way beyond the scope of what my father had meant when he used to say, "It takes all kinds."

Four years after Perot's daughter and her intended closed the deal with no incident, it became clear that one sort of wedding that most Americans did not want to become accustomed to — at least in the eyes of politicians who were trying to anticipate the desires of the voters as the 1996 elections approached — was a wedding between two people of the same sex. Even before a judge in Hawaii had ruled that such weddings could not be barred in that state, Newt Gingrich, the Speaker of the House, had said that if his half sister, a lesbian, married another woman he would not attend the ceremony. In other words, he publicly turned down an invitation that he hadn't been sent to a hypothetical event that could not legally take place. Bob Dole sponsored an anti-gay-marriage bill and Bill Clinton announced his willingness to sign it. When it came to the issue of gay marriage, bipartisanism was flourishing.

The press coverage about all of this got me to thinking about gay marriage for the first time, and I realized that I had one hypothetical objection to it, at least in its Jewish version. At the end of a gay Jewish wedding ceremony, how would you decide who stomps on the glass? The groom's breaking of a glass is a joyous part of the Jewish wedding ceremony, often followed by the assembled guests shouting "Mazel tov!" What if the ceremony ended with, instead of a confident stomp by the groom, some not so subtle maneuvering as each participant tried to put himself into position to be the one who did the stomping? There's a shoulder in the chest here and an elbow in the ribs — both by people who are ostensibly standing before a rabbi in a sober and respectful and loving frame of mind. Maybe somebody loses his temper. Maybe tension along the aisle separating the two sets of friends and relatives erupts into some shoving. (Why should the two families like each other simply because the people getting married are of the same sex?) Maybe somebody throws a punch that goes off course and knocks off the rabbi's glasses. What kind of way to begin a marriage is that? A concern about who would stomp on the glass might have appeared to be a trivial objection on my part — compared, say, to objections based on the belief that recognizing gay marriage would destroy civilization as we know it — but we all deal with these issues on our own level.

Then, by chance, Alice and I went to a perfectly legal heterosexual wedding in a synagogue in Chicago — the wedding of some friends of Abigail's we'd become close to while the bride and Abigail were in law school together. At the end of the ceremony, both the groom and the bride stomped on glasses. Apparently, that's done a lot these days. The solution to the problem of how a gay wedding would avoid fisticuffs over which partner broke the glass was there before our eyes: two glasses. I was, of course, greatly relieved. Gay marriage could go back to being one prospective societal phenomenon I didn't have to concern myself with, at least until the next presidential election.

I had simply been behind the times. I thought we'd been attending weddings at pretty much the same pace we'd always attended weddings—some of our friends were considerate enough to get married a few times in order to liven up that gap that usually occurs between the weddings of your contemporaries and the weddings of your contemporaries' children—but apparently the two-glass stomp was not the only development that had taken place without my notice. In the summer of 1995, Alice and I were driving in Ireland, listening on the car radio to someone relating how she'd explained to her father that, as a matter of principle, she didn't want him to walk down the aisle with her at her wedding; she was offended by the notion that one man was "giving her away" to another man. As she went on with the details of how she sat Daddy down in the parlor and explained all of this to him as diplomatically as possible, I began to hear some loud booing in the car, and gradually realized that it was coming from me. When I was able to stop booing, I said, "Not have her father walk down the aisle with her! What kind of talk is that! I thought the Church in Ireland was supposed to exercise a decent level of censorship over that kind of blather!"

Alice explained that many brides took care of the problem by simply walking down the aisle with both parents.

"Both parents?"

"Yes, both parents," Alice said.

"Is that legal?"

"I believe that in most states it's now legal," she said.

"But you'll be crying," I said. "How am I supposed to walk

down the aisle smiling proudly at my daughter if you're crying on the other side of her. It wouldn't be seemly."

Alice always cries at weddings. She cries even if the match being sanctified has long been spoken of as one that is unlikely to have much of a future. If the groom is well known as a cad, she cries anyway. While Alice is crying, I make mental notes for the review I always do of the ceremony in the car later. I notice that the flower arrangements are particularly attractive or that the minister can't seem to get the bride's name straight or that the stepmother seems to have a larger role than might have been expected or that the person who played the flute must have come cheap. During a longish wedding ceremony, with no more notes to make because the review will obviously be dominated by the sheer length of the proceedings, I sometimes pass the time trying to think of a man and a woman so loathsome that Alice would not be tempted to cry at their wedding.

If the truth be told, Alice sometimes cries at school plays. She has a weakness for any event that can be seen as one of life's landmarks. So think of how she'd cry at the wedding of one of her own daughters. Imagine the scene: Alice and I are walking down the aisle with a daughter in between us. The daughter has taken my arm, in the prescribed manner. Alice is dripping tears. I try to reach my free hand back to my pocket for the Kleenex supply, all the while keeping a joyful face on for the assembled. How am I going to get the Kleenex past the daughter in the middle? It seems inappropriate to hand the bride a few tissues and say, "Could you please pass these over? She's at it again."

As the scene flashed before my eyes, I was reminded of the quandary I found myself in when Abigail was born. It was a period when a lot of people — at least a lot of people we knew — went to natural childbirth classes. I had been in the labor room with Alice, doing contraction timing and light patter. There was Muzak in the labor room, and, seizing an opportunity to demonstrate the unfairness of what Alice always said about my lack of enthusiasm for ballroom dancing, I had invited her for a spin around the floor once or twice, during the slower fox-trots. All in all, I think I was in a cheerier mood than Alice was. When the obstetrician came in and said Alice was ready to go into the delivery room, he asked me if I'd like to come in for the birth. It seemed churlish to turn down the invitation. He led me to a locker room, where we both got into scrubs. Having heeded his warning not to leave my wallet in the locker with the rest of my clothing, I was holding it in my hand as we entered the delivery room; scrubs have no pockets. Then I realized that the elastic in the pants I'd been provided had about given out — I suppose it makes sense to use the older outfits for new fathers for a while, before throwing them away — so I had to hold up my pants with the other hand. As I neared the delivery table, Alice reached out to take my hand, as we had seen so many women do in the movies shown in natural childbirth classes. I had no hand available.

Was that scene going to repeat itself, more or less, at Abigail's wedding and Sarah's wedding? "It seems unnatural to have both parents," I said. "It's like a crowd moving down the aisle — a rugby team, or something. It's like having a bunch of people in the delivery room." An obstetrician we know says that these days it's not only the father of the baby who wants to attend the delivery. The mother's mother wants to be there, so, naturally, the mother's father feels that he should be there, too. Which means that his wife — who, of course, is someone completely different from the mother's mother—also wants to be there, more or less as protection for her husband. Then how about the baby's father's parents? They should not be present for the birth of their grandchild even though a perfect stranger—that's how they describe their daughter-in-law's stepmother—is there? Our obstetrician friend says that he has to kick people out of the delivery room all the time. "This is not a family picnic," he says. "This is not Thanksgiving dinner. This is not your Uncle Mortie's funeral. Get out of my delivery room."

"Abigail has no plans to get married right now," Alice said. "Neither does Sarah. Maybe we can wait to work it out when the time comes."

"First, I'd like to tell them the story of not having a spare hand in the delivery room," I said. "They have a right to know." It occurred to me, though, that they had probably heard that story already. I think it was one of the stories I used to tell them at breakfast.

13

New York, New York

t some point, Abigail got old enough to ask me why I routinely included her when I said to people we met that we were from Kansas City. "I was born in New York," she said. "And I've always lived in New York. So how can I be from Kansas City?"

I had an answer ready. I said, "If an American diplomat who is stationed in Paris has a child, the child is not French. The child is an American who happened to have been born in France. You are someone from Kansas City who happened to have been born in New York while your parents were living there." Somehow, though, I felt that my answer was unconvincing. It must have been apparent to Abigail by then that her parents had been living in New York for considerably longer than the customary diplomatic posting. It must have been apparent to her that her mother—who had been raised in Westchester County, New York, and was regularly referred to by me as a fancy Eastern girl — looked blank when I talked about the possibility of moving back home someday. ("We could always go home, Alice. I would buy you a house overlooking the brown waters of Lake Lotawana. The girls and I would go to the American Royal Livestock Show every year instead of to the Feast of St. Anthony. We could have another wedding reception, with all of the same relatives.") Looking at the situation realistically, I had to face the fact that I had arrived at yet another one of those moments that parents respond to with a mixture of pride and sadness: the kid is old enough to understand that on this subject the parent is, as my own father would have said, full of beans. A precursor to that landmark may be when the kid tosses one of your standard lines back to you. While I was preparing breakfast one morning, not long before this discussion of Abigail's Midwestern origins came up, she had asked me how I'd feel about something she wanted to do — I can't remember what — that involved a question of manners or appropriate dress, and I said that, although it sounded all right to me, I wasn't certain Alice would feel the same way.

"You mean because she's a fancy Eastern girl and you're just a simple lad from the Midwest?" Abigail asked.

I looked over at Abigail, who was pouring milk on her cereal. I thought I detected a small, sly smile.

"Well, yes, Abigail," I replied. "In fact, I couldn't have said it better myself."

I thought of myself as a sort of resident out-of-towner in New York — someone who appeared confident in the subway but had never actually penetrated the deepest secrets of the BMT line. There had already been indications that Abigail and Sarah would eventually move out of that category. When Abigail was only four or five, we took what I have persisted in calling a trip home, and Abigail asked, "Daddy, how come the bagels in Kansas City taste like just round bread?" This was years before bagel shops had begun to sprout in what New Yorkers would have considered the bagel barrens—parts of the country that social scientists with a bakery bent would categorize as white bread sorts of places. We were still in the era when people in a place like Kansas City who happened to eat a local bagel tended not to know that what they were eating was not a bagel but some sort of bagel-shaped, breadlike object. Abigail did know, just the way that little boy from New Orleans knew that the steamed white rice in the dining room of a Holiday Inn or a Best Western somewhere in Iowa did not taste the way rice was supposed to taste.

Most of the family rituals we took for granted were solidly grounded in New York. Looking back, I'm amazed by how many of them had to do with eating. Of course, it is common for New Yorkers to express their connection with the city in culinary terms. During the years Edward Koch was mayor of New York, the one moment when I felt unqualified empathy with him was when he said he had no intention of running for governor because there weren't any decent Chinese restaurants in Albany. (He changed his mind—about running for governor, not about the restaurants—and lost.) From almost the time the girls were born, I got in the habit of taking them on Sunday mornings to a line of stores on Houston Street, on the Lower East Side, to buy bagels at Tanenbaum's Bakery, creamed cheese and baked farmer's cheese at Ben's Dairy and, of course, smoked salmon at Russ & Daughters, an establishment I described at the time as "a splendid refutation of the false teaching that a store can't have character and a clean display case at the same time." When Abigail and Sarah were small, Russ &

Daughters was run by the daughters of the founder, Joel Russ, and their husbands. The arrival of my girls always caused a little stir; someone who had been concentrating on slicing salmon a moment earlier might emerge from behind the counter bearing a candy fish and expecting a hug. In those years, a friend of mine found a less expensive source of high-quality salmon—a smoker in the Canadian Maritimes who would fill orders by mail. When my friend informed me of his discovery, I had to tell him that I wasn't interested. "Is he going to come out to pinch their cheeks and give them candy?" I asked. "Is he going to tell me how adorable they are? There are certain services you can't perform by mail."

On Saturday mornings, I often put Sarah on the back of my bike and rode over to the Greenmarket in the West Village. Or I walked with Abigail to Joe's Dairy, on Sullivan Street, for some mozzarella. The annual St. Anthony Feast on Sullivan was traditionally our last big New York event before we left for Nova Scotia. In the fall, we usually went to the San Gennaro festival, on Mulberry Street. In both places, I would have to spend a good deal of my time trying to work through the difficult selection process involved in choosing the one sausage sandwich—hot Italian sausage, accompanied by fried onions and peppers—that I was going to allow myself at each festival as my entire annual consumption of that delicacy. ("Somehow, it has been clear to me since I came to the city that uncontrolled, year-round eating of sausage sandwiches is not an acceptable option for me," I wrote during those years. "It was instinct more than conscious decision—the sort of instinct that some animals must use to know how many of certain berries to eat in the woods.") The girls, munching on *zeppole* that were almost pure white from powdered sugar, would patiently stroll up and down the street with me as I carried out my inspections.

Once, when Sarah was in high school, she and some of her friends were at our house for a meal that we had picked up in a few different restaurants in Chinatown. Sarah, like Abigail before her, had gone from IS 70 to a private school uptown. (I haven't offered advice to parents trying to decide among private schools in New York, but I have made one observation: About all you can do is pick the school whose parent body offends you the least.) We were merrily devouring our dinner—in between observations of who in the school was a total dweeb and who was stupid crazy and who was crazy stupid, plus discussions of who at the table might get through a sentence or two without using the word "like," as in "I was like 'like what?' And he was like 'like O.K.' "—when one of the young men present (I'll call him Trevor, since that has always been an underutilized name in New York) said that, even though he was truly enjoying what he was eating, it didn't actually taste like Chinese food to him. Under close questioning, it turned out that what Trevor thought Chinese food tasted like was that tired glop delivered to your door by neighborhood Chinese restaurants connected to the brown-sauce pipe that, according to legend, runs just underground all over Manhattan.

"This is what Chinese food tastes like in Chinatown," Sarah said.

Trevor said that, although he had lived in New York all of his life, he had never been to Chinatown. Sarah looked at him as if he'd just said that he was gradually coming to a new appreciation of the music of Guy Lombardo and His Royal Canadians. I was astonished myself. Trevor had grown up on the Upper East Side, so it wouldn't have surprised me at all to find that the cultural opportunities offered him had been rather narrow. But never been to Chinatown! I hardly knew how to respond to a case of deprivation that, to my mind, bordered on abuse. Trevor must have been about seventeen — too old to be placed with a kindly foster family in some other part of the city.

Chinatown had always been a part of what we did as a family, and not just on Thanksgiving. It was an obvious place to have dinner with another family, since restaurants in Chinatown have an attitude toward children that is the precise opposite of those tea parlors in England where the hostess flashes an icy smile at the children and says, "Aren't they dear," and seats your party as far away from civilized guests as possible. ("Baby bigot approaching," I used to mutter to Alice when we encountered one of those. About the warmest statement regarding children I've run across in an English restaurant was on a table-card I brought home from East Anglia: "Children are welcome on the basis that they do not disturb other customers or cause damage to themselves or others.") In Chinatown proprietors and patrons take it for granted that you might want to bring the kids along and that kids make noise. I can remember our goddaughter, Caroline Smith, at the age of two or three, pounding on a table with a spoon in a Chinatown restaurant as she yelled, "More Chinese food! More Chinese food!" None of the other diners seemed to notice. There are nearly always Chinese kids in the restaurant — looking relaxed, I've thought since I read the data of that Massachusetts social scientist, partly because they don't have to worry about some grown-up reminding them that it's past their bedtime and hustling them off to a dark room.

For years, we've been walking to Chinatown for lunch. The custom began as a way of showing out-of-town visitors some of lower Manhattan. Starting out in the Village, we'd walk through the Italian South Village, through Soho, through what I usually describe as an awkward block or two in the machine tool district, through Little Italy, and finally to Chinatown, where we'd have a dim sum lunch and then repair to the Chinese Amusement Arcade so that the visitor would have the opportunity to play tic-tac-toe with a live chicken. As the girls got into high school and college, walking to Chinatown became a way of taking a sort of urban outing with them and their friends. A crowd of Sarah's friends or Abigail's friends — or, eventually, a mixture of the two — would gather at our house and then we'd set off for what was always a huge, jolly lunch. It's about a twenty-five-minute walk if you avoid stops along the way, which, I'm pleased to say, we have almost never done: to sustain ourselves on the journey, we tend to stop on Sullivan Street for mozzarella and on Mott Street for grilled Chinese radish cakes at the very least.

Although we consciously went light on the chicken feet, the girls' friends tended to be pretty adventurous — except for a young man we have since referred to as the shrimp detector. He was just beginning rabbinical seminary in Los Angeles. It wasn't an Orthodox seminary. He assured us that he had no problem with eating in a nonkosher restaurant, as long as he stayed away from pork and shellfish. That sounded like a reasonable enough compromise, except that he could spot shrimp in microscopic amounts. He was a cheerful enough young man. When I said, "I suppose they hit you with a required course in shrimp detection as part of the orientation in that place — figuring the Torah and that sort of thing can wait for a semester or two," he just smiled and continued his examination of some stuffed eggplant. For a moment, I thought he was going to take out a jeweler's loupe. The girls' favorite dish at dim sum restaurants happens to be shrimp wrapped in lasagna-sized rice noodles and doused with sauce; for some reason, they've always called it slime. They are also partial to chive dumplings that, because of their shape, we refer to as hockey pucks. Toward the end of the meal, I saw the shrimp detector turn a hockey puck from side to side and stare suspiciously at what he apparently believed to be a speck of pork; he was a study in the perils of trying to take a middle course. Sarah offered to eat the hockey puck for him, just in case.

By the time the girls were in high school, they were considered old enough to participate in the sort of Chinese-food-gathering operation that had provided dinner for Trevor—what we have always called the Entebbe raid. It was named, of course, for the lightning strike of Israeli commandos that freed airline hostages held at an airport in Uganda in 1976. Our version of the Entebbe raid was based on the common-sense assumption that, as long as you were going to bring in food from Chinatown for a bunch of people, there was no reason to limit yourself to one restaurant. After one or two restaurants had been alerted by phone to begin preparing their specialties, Abigail and Sarah and I and sometimes one of the guests would pile into the car. In Chinatown, the raiders, their watches synchronized and their assignments made absolutely clear by instructions during the drive, would fan out from the car to snare a dish or two from a number of different restaurants — say, pepper and salty shrimp at an old Cantonese favorite of ours, some of the cold dishes in the window from one of the Shanghainese places, deboned duck feet with jellyfish from a new discovery. Then, quarry in hand, we'd make the dash back to the Village, arriving with the mission's objective still hot in little white containers. There were times when we entered to applause.

In the eighties, the New York Public Library began holding

a biannual event called the Tables of Content dinners—nearly a hundred volunteer hosts throwing dinner parties on the same night to raise money for the library. The dinners, described in the invitation so that the paying guests could decide which one to sign up for, included bashes like "A Monticello Memory" ("A salute to the great gourmet Thomas Jefferson, with some of the foods he introduced to the United States—and music of the period") and "Dinner with Edward VII" ("A formal twelve-course dinner featuring the King's favorite dishes") and a fifteenth-century French Christmas banquet ("Guests will dine on the cuisine of the great chef Taillevent. Menu: Brouet d'Allemagne, porcelet, rosty, galimafrée de mouton, and venaisin") and an evening devoted to old Vienna ("A six-course dinner celebrating turn-of-the-century Vienna and Secessionist painter Gustav Klimt in the presence of His Excellency the Ambassador of Austria and Mrs. Klestil") and "A Raj Banquet at Princely Hyderabad" and a dinner called simply "Anna Karenina" ("Feast on dozens of oysters, relish the turbot, savor the soup, sample the champagne and revel in the lavish style of prerevolutionary Russia as you relive Levin and Oblonsky's splendid dinner at Angleterre in Moscow"). When we were asked to host one of the dinners so that I could write about it in a book the library was going to publish, we knew we'd have an Entebbe raid. We offered to have fourteen guests at a dinner listed in the invitation as "Pretty Decent Chinese Take-out." The descriptive paragraph was "No eating directly from the carton allowed."

I don't remember ever mentioning Chinatown on trips back to Kansas City when I was asked how I could be raising kids in New York. In those years, the stress and dirt and crime of New York were staples on late-night television shows. I had gradually developed a one-sentence answer to the questions my high school friends always asked about how I could bear living there myself: There are no chiggers in New York. That happens to be literally true. There are any number of New Yorkers who don't even know that such a thing as a chigger exists. When you try to explain, they often begin to get the idea that it is some completely imaginary creature that is used by outlanders to josh city people, the snipe of the bug family. (It doesn't help matters that an honest description of the chigger has to begin with the fact that it is not visible to the human eye.) Chiggers do exist in the Midwest and South. I wouldn't say that their distribution coincides precisely with the bagel barrens, but there is a strong overlap. In Kansas City, dread of chiggers is strong—as well it might be, since the itch power of a single chigger bite has been gauged (by me) as the equivalent of eight thousand mosquito bites. My information about New York's not having chiggers would usually end any discussion about why a sentient human being would choose to live there.

It would not end a discussion about why you might want to raise a family there. Years later, Speaker of the House Newt Gingrich—whose authoritative tone on family matters presumably comes from something other than personal experience—said that New Yorkers have "no concept of families." Even before New York became the easiest shorthand for the problems of American cities, people in the rest of the country assumed that it was an odd place to bring up kids. Had we at least given serious consideration to a move to the suburbs? "Moving to the suburbs would be unfair to the children," I always said. "It would be harmful to them to be raised partly by someone in the mood I'd be in if I lived in the suburbs." Also, any big-city perils a New York parent can imagine seemed to me to pale in comparison to the thought of your children being in a car operated by a teenaged American boy. While growing up in the suburbs of New York, Alice put in a fair amount of time riding in cars operated by teenaged American boys, and she emerged speaking of the experience in the tone of someone who came through the London blitz—survival by luck of the draw. Compared to a teenaged American boy, a New York taxi driver, even one who is newly arrived from Bangladesh or Haiti and still slightly confused about the circumstances under which a U-turn is legal, seems like a trusted old family retainer.

I've never come up with a simple phrase that encompasses what there is to cherish about raising kids in New York. If I did, I think it would be a variation of what some friends of ours who spent a few years in India say when they're told by Americans that it must have been terribly difficult and stressful raising small children there. On the contrary, they say, it was like being at a circus twenty-four hours a day. The kids were constantly enthralled. They might pass a snake charmer on the way to school or see an elephant pass by while they were playing in the garden. I have to acknowledge that snake charmers and strolling elephants would both have to be included if I made a list of exotica that I haven't run across in all of my years in New York. On the other hand, it would be a short list.

"But wasn't it scary to raise children in New York?" I'm asked on trips home. "Weren't you always worried about them?"

Of course I was always worried about them. I would have been worried about them if we lived in a peaceful farming hamlet in Indiana. Parents worry. I think most parents agree that you worry less about children who have grown up, left home, and live in another city. Basically, though, I believe that the only time parents are absolutely relaxed about the safety and well-being of their child, of any age, is when that child is under the parents' own roof, fast asleep.

At the very least, parents wonder whether they *should* worry. I always found it comforting when I'd come across something I could decide not to worry about. Then I could cross it off the list. When Sarah was little, she had an imaginary friend named Craig Binnger. "Imaginary friends are supposed to have names like Jack or Popo or Tillie-bear," I said to Alice. "How come her friend sounds like a life-insurance salesman?" Should we worry about that? No. Should we worry about summers in Nova Scotia depriving our girls of the experience of summer camp, where they might learn to play games and torment weaker children? No. At one time, a psychology professor figured out that a five-foot-two, 125-pound woman who wanted to have pretty much the same proportions that a Barbie doll has would have to grow two feet taller, add five inches to her chest and lose six inches from her waist—meaning that little girls familiar with Barbie dolls could get an unrealistic notion of the ideal body. Should we worry about that? Let's not. It once dawned on me that when we took long trips in the car our girls were not arguing about who was on whose side of the backseat. When I was a child, our family often took long trips in the car, and Sukey and I had an invisible line drawn down the middle of the backseat. (At least *she* said it was the middle.) Incursions drew what I believe the foreign policy people call a strong response. I've written about this. I've talked about it in public, and when I do I see people nodding their heads. Sukey and I were obviously not the only siblings who had tension on the border. Why was there no sound of a strong response from the backseat of our car? Should I worry about the possibility of an absence of contentiousness that could disable them in a world

organized more or less like a New York delicatessen line? I
decided not to. I decided to cross that off the list of things to
worry about.

Did one of the worries that remained on my list have to do
with the girls not being from Kansas City? Maybe. It took me
a number of years to acknowledge that they were New Yorkers.
When they were small, we often took them to Kansas City.
Sometimes, they would stay with my mother and Sukey while
Alice and I continued on to someplace we had reason to believe
was short on Pampers or sanitation. Our intentions went beyond
the obvious convenience of leaving our girls with loving and
trustworthy babysitters. For one thing, our only extended family
was in Kansas City—Alice's family in the East, which wasn't
large to begin with, had more or less evaporated—and we
thought it was good for the girls to spend some time included
in it. But, I admitted at the time, I also saw a trip home as
amounting to a sort of booster shot in Kansas City ways. Before
we had kids, Alice and I both found something off-putting in
New York kids we heard about who seemed not just over-
privileged but oversavvy—the sort of kids who, in sixth grade,
had not only been to any number of chic resorts but had also
organized the primary turnout for Eugene McCarthy in their
neighborhood and founded a small radio station. We had both
had upbringings whose essential squareness we valued, and I
thought of mine in geographical terms. In the book I wrote
about my father, I suggested that most childhoods turn out
to have themes if you look hard enough—a theme like "Our
family has a distinguished heritage that you must live up to"
or a theme like "We are suffering because your father deserted
us"—and I acknowledged that, looking back on it, the theme
I was hoping our daughters' childhood in Greenwich Village

had was "Despite all evidence to the contrary, you are being raised in Kansas City."

There was, I admit, a lot of evidence to the contrary. Eventually, Abigail and Sarah were privy to the sort of information that New Yorkers keep from out-of-towners, even out-of-towners who have lived in the city for thirty or forty years. On the subways, for instance, their instinctive knowledge of what all of those letters and numbers on the trains mean would make them comfortable putting together combinations that were more than just straight shots on the IRT. They would know all the secrets of the BMT, almost as if by intuition. They would know where in the train to stand to get off near the stairway they were going to be using to get to the next train. "No, we should be in the back car," they would say to their father, guiding him in the way that the children of immigrants sometimes guide parents who are a little slower in picking up the language. In certain ways, I have to admit, Abigail and Sarah are from New York.

14

Nova Scotia

The puzzlement of people in Kansas City as to why we would choose to live in New York was nothing compared with the usual response of New Yorkers to learning that we spent our summers in Nova Scotia. Over the years, it has been impressed upon me that a lot of Americans—including some with advanced degrees—don't know where Nova Scotia is. A lot of them don't know that it's a province of Canada, and those who do usually have it mixed up with Newfoundland. Most Americans appear to know that Canada is to the north of the United States, but that may be mainly because it is always identified as where cold fronts come from. After living in Nova Scotia part-time for a quarter of a century or so, our family has come to think of itself as just a little bit Canadian. In fact, I've suggested from time to time that for purposes of what's known as Canadian Content—the presence of Canadian artists or actors or writers in a project as part of the government's effort to keep Canada from being overwhelmed by American culture—someone who lives in Canada during July and August every year might be considered one-twelfth Canadian. For every six books on the Canadiana shelf by Margaret Atwood, there could be one of mine. So far, the response of the Canadian authorities to that suggestion has been pretty much the same as Alice's response to my thoughts about moving back home and buying her a house overlooking the brown waters of Lake Lotawana. Still, I remain a Canada booster. I believe I continue to hold the record for consecutive columns by an American columnist on Canada: two.

We have been able to live in Nova Scotia in the summer because, from the time the girls were tiny, we enjoyed a privilege that faxes and computers and high-speed modems are now said to be making available to more and more Americans: Alice and I both did the kind of work that did not require daily attendance at an office. Even in New York, we often worked at home at the same time, close enough for me to shout for help if I wanted to use a word I couldn't seem to spell. The girls took it for granted that they'd probably find a parent or two hanging around the house when they got home from school. I would save up the long pieces of writing I had to do for the summer. Alice, who eventually went from academia to producing educational films, would normally be able to juggle projects around to avoid having to be in New York in July or August. One Sunday evening in August, when Sarah was maybe seven or eight, we were driving toward our house in Nova Scotia from the Halifax airport, after having dropped off some guests, and I noticed quite a bit of traffic—at least quite a bit of traffic for Nova Scotia—coming in our direction. "Must be Halifax people with houses on the shore coming back from the weekend," I said.

"Why are they going back?" Sarah asked, from the backseat.

"Because it's Sunday night."

"Yes, but why are they going back?"

"Because it's Sunday night, Sarah."

"But it's summertime," Sarah said. "There's no school to-morrow."

There was a long pause. "Sarah," I finally said. "There's something we should have told you about a long time ago. On Monday morning, many people go to offices and facto-ries . . ."

At around the end of June every year, we simply moved our base of operations to Nova Scotia. Packing the car was the cul-mination of what we called the Leaving Frenzy—the arrange-ments and chores and checklists necessary to leave the city for a couple of months. On the official departure day, I would get the car, usually a Volkswagen with a roof rack, from the lot and park it in the front of the house. Everything that was supposed to be going to Nova Scotia had been brought out on the side-walk from a staging area in the house we called Cam Ranh Bay, after the United States Army's largest supply depot in South Vietnam. The girls sat on the stoop to watch—and, in later years, to make disrespectful remarks about my packing techniques. Sometimes, a small crowd of neighbors gathered. I always suspected that they made small side bets on whether I'd actually get everything in (or on top of) the car, which soon took on the look of a space capsule. I don't know which way I would have bet. One year, when Alice had some meetings in New York she had to stay for, the girls and I drove up without her and she went by plane. "We'll miss you on the drive up, of course," I told her, "but frankly we're grateful for your cubic feet."

On one of the first few journeys to Nova Scotia—when the

Leaving Frenzy had been particularly exhausting and the roof rack held not only two or three huge suitcases but a couple of boxes of light fixtures, all secured with a tarp and bungee cords — we were driving at about fifty miles an hour on the West Side Highway, fifteen minutes from our departure point, when the entire roof rack took leave of the car. Fortunately, there was nobody immediately behind us. With the suitcases and boxes still tightly bound to the rack, the entire package bounced on the pavement, took two or three flips, and landed upright on the West Side Highway. I screeched to a halt. Cars were swerving around the roof rack and our car as if on a slalom course. Alice and I sat numbly in the front seat as if we'd been pole-axed. Before we could think of something appropriate to say — maybe "woe is us" — a New York police car pulled up behind us, its light flashing. A huge policeman got out. He and I walked back to look at our possessions. He didn't seem at all surprised to see a roof rack on the West Side Highway. I don't know why so many cops in New York are so much less rigid and tense than policemen in other cities. I suppose you could argue that they've seen everything — the cops in the Sixth Precinct have even seen a person turn an unmarked twenty-dollar bill into lost and found — but I have always been tempted by an old theory that they gain great security from being in a position to make their arrest quota anytime they want to.

"I think if you back the car up, and I take one side of this thing and you take the other side, we can put it back on," he said. That approach to the problem had not actually occurred to me. It worked. In another minute, with the roof rack secured well enough to make it as far as a garage, we were back on our way to Nova Scotia. Ever since then, Alice has referred to the roof rack as an example of how difficulties that seem overwhelming—from a seemingly endless house renovation to a course of radiation—will eventually be resolved. I suspect she would argue for "Remember the Roof Rack" as a family motto, although I've always thought that we could make do with what I've finally deduced must have been the motto of my family when I was growing up in Kansas City—"Zip Up Your Jacket."

We hadn't expected to find ourselves with a house in Nova Scotia. When we were first married and Alice was on an academic schedule, she'd come with me in the summer on projects that had been chosen partly for their location—a report for the Peace Corps in Africa one summer, a couple of stories in the South Pacific the summer after that. When we began thinking about where to go the first summer of Abigail's life, 1969, places like Africa and the South Pacific were not in contention. We did want to spend the summer somewhere out of the country. In 1969, a lot of people were feeling the need for at least a brief respite from the United States of America. We wanted to be able to bring some baby supplies, and, as new parents, we wanted to be in a place that didn't seem terribly foreign when it came to, say, pediatricians and pharmacists. Partly because we had friends in Toronto who hoped to join up with us, renting a house in the Canadian Maritimes seemed about right. That's how Alice and Abigail and I came to be taking a drive late in a summer we had spent on the South Shore of Nova Scotia and happening upon a village we particularly liked—a string of houses on a harbor of the Atlantic, with a fleet of fishing boats and a couple of small fish-buying operations and two lighthouses. As it turned out, there was a dilapidated house for sale.

On the morning we woke up after spending our first night in the house—this was three years later, after we had finally hired a local contractor to make it habitable—Alice raised the shade and said, "There's a cow in the front yard." A neighbor who had been asked by the contractor to take the hay had shown up with his oxcart and his scythe. We were a long way from Greenwich Village. People on the South Shore of Nova Scotia have a characteristic way of talking, and it was much stronger then, particularly among the older residents. Their best-known locution was the use of a few words as adverbs that you didn't often hear used as adverbs elsewhere—"some," for instance, and "Jesus." It used to be said that a South Shore child who was asked to decline "good" would say, instead of "good, better, best," something like "good, some good, and right some goddamn Jesus good." I've heard people in our town talk about a low tide that is not just low but "wicked Jesus low." When Abigail was three or so, the response of one older neighbor to meeting her was "She's some cunning." A little girl who was playing with Abigail around that time responded to one of my lame jokes by looking up at me and saying, in a friendly enough sort of way, "You're some 'tupid."

I loved the idea of spending the summer in a place that was far removed from our lives during the rest of the year. The girls had to learn that certain activities could be done only at high tide and certain activities only at low (for getting clams or mussels, a wicked Jesus low was even better than just low). Given the capacity of our well, they had to learn that there was some relationship between rainfall and the amount of water available in the tap. On dry summers, we'd talk a lot about what might be done about the water supply. I was eventually inspired to write a little fable about a married couple whose Augusts—the only time they were truly together, since both were caught up in their careers the other eleven months—were spent discussing what to do about the well at their summer cottage. When they finally got a new well, it became apparent that they had nothing else to talk about, and they got a divorce. Until we finally got a new well, I would appoint myself chairman of the Water Committee in dry summers and would trust no one else to wash the dishes. Years later, Alice would sometimes say that I'd never gotten over the chairmanship of the Water Committee — even though I no longer insisted on being called Mr. Chairman while at the kitchen sink.

Eventually, of course, the South Shore began to change. The use of "some" as an adverb became less common. (The people in our area remained as imaginative as ever in their use of words like "into" and "onto," though, so that I continued to get a warm confirmation of being back every summer the first time I heard something like "He built a bungalow with a picture window into it" or "That haddock had an awful smell onto it.") Sooner or later, the South Shore became a place where oxcarts were rare and exotic foodstuffs like olive oil might be found in certain supermarkets. But it remained a place where the rhythm of our lives was completely different. In a poem Abigail wrote in high school as part of a birthday present to me, she described it as a place where "the most complicated problem to be solved / Is when to make the bread / So as to be able to go out in the boat at high tide / But still have bread for dinner." In Nova Scotia, I found myself doing tasks I'd never thought about doing in New York — fileting fish, for instance, or building stone walls. I'd actually try to fix things. I'd make a try at shoving the foot pedal farther down in the well with an old eel-spear. I'd devote some time to unjamming the line on the brush cutter. In New York one evening, someone we were having dinner with asked what it was like in Nova Scotia, and Alice said that I was a different person there.

"Alice," I said. "There's something I've been meaning to tell you. When we go through Maine on the way up, I change places with another guy, then I go back to New York and spend my time writing and drinking beer."

"I like the other guy better," Alice said.

In the first couple of summers we had the house, when the girls were still babies, I suppose I took it for granted that the reason we lived on the South Shore in the summer was largely economic. In those days, Nova Scotia was a place where people who didn't think they could buy a summer house could buy a summer house, as long as they didn't have to be within shooting distance of the office. I couldn't see the role Nova Scotia would play in our lives, partly because I always had trouble envisioning our children at any age other than the age they were right at the time. As it turned out, the real reason we lived in Nova Scotia was that it was a place where we could have the girls to ourselves. Although it was nice that our town was on the shore, its most important characteristic was that it was out of our orbit. Alice and Abigail and Sarah and I were the summer community. When the girls were small, we hired a babysitter about once a summer. On those nights, Alice and I would drive to the nearest movie theater, usually to find that the movie we thought was playing had been replaced—sometimes, I swear, during the time we were on the highway—by a comedy starring Don Knotts.

Once we got to Nova Scotia, I almost never went back to the United States until we all returned after Labor Day. Occasionally, Alice would have to go back for a meeting, and the girls sometimes kept notes about what we did during her absence, so they could fill her in later. Meals during those periods tended to be dominated by Kool-Aid, beer, and Kraft macaroni-

and-cheese dinner. An entry in the notes about a meal like that would have next to it "CAMP"—cats away, mice play. Some summers, friends came to visit. We sometimes got together with families that lived nearby. But Nova Scotia was mainly just us, in a way that a city where we all had our own schedules could never have been. When Alice wrote about her illness herself, it was in an article called "Of Dragons and Garden Peas" that appeared in the *New England Journal of Medicine,* and the garden peas she talked about getting back to when she escaped from "the land of the sick people" were in Nova Scotia. Although we only spent two months a year in the Nova Scotia house, all of us saw it, I think, as the equivalent of what Midwestern farm families mean when they talk about the home place.

I never knew quite what to tell people who asked how we occupied ourselves in Nova Scotia. Abigail's theory was that we spent our time looking for dinner—finding a fisherman who had brought in some halibut or searching the woods for mushrooms or going out to an island in the harbor to collect mussels or checking crab traps or digging up potatoes. We had a lot of picnics. We went to a lot of fairs. We attended a lot of the community suppers that Alice used to refer to as the Annual Starch Festival.

Nova Scotia was also where we made most of our movies—at least the musicals. Our earliest movies were made with friends we were visiting in the West of England. I had a silent camera then, not much different from the one my father used during my childhood to record family picnics or trips to the West. My father's standard pictures were of people standing in a line, giggling and waving self-consciously; presumably at a command from the photographer, they would suddenly walk toward the camera. We didn't make any waving-and-walking movies. Even before we got into talkies, we made movies with plots. Alice would use a little film splicer to edit what we'd shot on the silent camera, and then I'd add a narrative that never seemed quite in sync with what was on the screen. To make a film we needed another family or a convenient supply of assorted children, in order to have enough actors for the major roles. Grown-ups were limited to bit parts, usually foolish bit parts. The robber with the foxlike grin who stole the golden egg in the movie cited by the inspector from the Responsible Parenting League, for instance, was played by a little boy named Danny Jowell. The rather dense stableman so easily tricked by the robber was played by Danny's father. It is probably unnecessary for me to name the actresses who were typecast as what the credits called "two lovely little girls."

Eventually, we turned to a sound camera, but we never graduated to video technology. It didn't seem amenable to the type of editing we required. Also, we had no use for any technology that wouldn't include the capacity to show the finished product on an old sheet in our barn every summer at what we called the annual South Shore Film Festival. The festival had the same subtitle every year: A Trillin Retrospective. The girls and Alice would spend the afternoon making lemonade and baking cookies; I'd lay in a supply of beer for the rougher elements. Our one rule was a sort of flip on the policy of those theaters that won't let customers in after a mystery has started: if you were there when our movies started, you weren't allowed to leave. Given the entertainment opportunities along the South Shore of Nova Scotia in those days, the South Shore Film Festival was always well attended, although I'll admit that there was a certain amount of grumbling over the no-leaving policy.

The feature presentation was whatever movie we had made the previous summer — say, *It's So Crazy It Just Might Work.* One of the features had a title reflecting the fact that many people in New York would tend to identify Nova Scotia as a type of smoked salmon rather than as a province of Canada; it was called *If There's No Nova Scotia in Nova Scotia, There Can't Be Any French Fries in France.* That one was about two high-powered New York hostesses who were competing to find a smoked salmon source that would be as special as the source they had for every other ingredient they used ("I've got my own little man," one of them sang. "He gets for me some unusual tea that's made by some monks in Japan. Japan is where monk tea began"). It also featured a fish smoker whose ambitions in the country music field were reflected in a song called "Smokin' Fish Just Ain't My Dish; I Wanna Be a Star" and a fisherman who, using the local construction, sings a song entitled "By God, These Tourists Are Some Dumb" (". . . they don't eat supper 'til near half past nine. They'd buy your boot if they thought it was pine").

In the musicals, Sarah played, among other roles, one of the competing New York hostesses and, in *Yech,* a woman from New Jersey who has a nearly religious devotion to the Paramus Mall. Abigail's most memorable star turn was in *Yech*; outfitted in a beret and a French accent, she played the niece of Hercule Poirot investigating the murder of a visiting mushroom authority. The story line would usually emerge from discussions around the dinner table. Lyrics would be learned. The tune would be recorded on a tape recorder that could be hidden behind a bush to accompany the actor. Since we usually didn't have anybody around who could write music, I would borrow the tunes for our songs — many from composers whose musicals we had watched at St. Bart's and the Equity Library Theater. Like any good thief, I tried to disguise the origin of the tunes by writing lyrics that weren't at all parallel to the original, hoping that "By God, These Tourists Are Some Dumb" would not be instantly identifiable as "That's Why the Lady Is a Tramp" or that the tune of "I'm Always True to You, Darling, in My Fashion" would be sort of blended away in the song called "Uncle Max's Kids Are Gross, Creepy, Dumb and Yucky."

One June, just a day or two before we were about to leave for Nova Scotia, I got a call from someone who said he was doing a story for a Canadian magazine on American summer communities in Canada, and was interested in the writers' colony I lived in on the South Shore. "Either you're having a little joke with me or someone's having a little joke with you," I said. I told him that a close friend of ours, who was employed as a librarian in the high school nearest to our town, was married to an American and was working on a South Shore cookbook, but that didn't seem to me to qualify as the sort of activity magazine editors have in mind when they talk about American writers' colonies.

"There must have been some misunderstanding," he said. "We had heard that you all made films during the summer and then had a festival where everyone showed his film."

I'm afraid my voice grew rather severe. "No one's movies are permitted at the South Shore Film Festival except *our* movies," I said. "The subtitle is *always* 'A Trillin Retrospective.'"

15

A Place for the Wedding

In 1995, *The New York Times* reported that the percentage of brides who took their husbands' names seemed to be going up slightly. That squared with the impression I'd gathered from my perusal every Sunday of the *Times* wedding and engagement announcements. I've had an almost scholarly interest in the announcements for years. A long time ago, I admitted publicly that I read about the bride and the groom and their families so carefully because I like to imagine the tension at the reception. It's not the sort of thing I'm proud of, but there you are. For a while, a friend of mine had a Sunday *Times* society page addiction similar to mine, and when the phone rang late on a Sunday morning I knew the voice on the other end might be saying something like "I'm assuming that late in the otherwise flawless reception that Mr. and Mrs. Hopkins Tidwell arranged for the wedding of their daughter, the debutante Blake Tidwell, the bridegroom's father, T. J. O'Malley, of the

Transit Authority O'Malleys, is not going to absolutely insist on doing the rendition of 'Danny Boy' that wowed everyone last year toward the end of the Knights of Columbus Christmas bash."

To which, on my very best day, I might be able to answer, "If the Tidwells try to put on society airs, I assume Mr. O'Malley will make it clear that he knows that the cotillion Miss Tidwell was presented at can be bought at deep discount, which also happens to be true of admission to that college for airheads she went to. I suspect O'Malley's too well brought up to mention the fact that the fancy-sounding investment bank Mr. Tidwell is a senior partner of seems to be having a bit of trouble lately with the Securities and Exchange Commission."

My interest in wedding announcements began in the sixties. In those days, the announcements seemed dominated by debutantes. Unlikely as it may seem, I'd had some exposure to debutantes when I was an undergraduate. In Eastern universities, it was common for students of tweedy background—the people I have always embodied in a roommate I call Thatcher Baxter Hatcher—to haul Midwestern high school boys along to debutante parties on Long Island and Connecticut estates. My knowledge of the subject was greatly refined through the vagaries of general assignment reporting. While working at the New York bureau of *Time*, I was assigned to look into the debutante industry—the caterers and dance bands and society dancing teachers and, most important for what was to become my priority Sunday morning reading, the consultants who could help take the shine off new money by shoehorning a daughter into certain cotillions. I learned in the process why the parents of debutantes, who would be expected to be intensely concerned about the bloodlines of their children's friends, were so casual about opening the door to unknown college boys from the boondocks: apparently, the need for males at such events was so acute that just about anyone who had a tuxedo and a pulse was welcome.

Not long after I finished my assignment, I happened to glance at the wedding announcements one Sunday and realized that I could tell which one of the newly engaged young women whose pictures were shown had come out at a debutante cotillion that could be bought and which at a cotillion that was authentically snotty. The rest of the information needed for making distinctions between the backgrounds of the bride and groom was more or less at hand already—knowledge about the academic standards of various colleges and the animosity between various ethnic groups and the standing of various law firms and investment banks. I discovered that I could interpret wedding announcements in the way that literary critics can deconstruct a passage of poetry or that Kremlinologists in the Cold War era could extract some meaning out of who was standing where on the Kremlin's reviewing stand at the May Day parade.

Beginning in the late sixties, an arcane knowledge of cotillion rankings became less and less valuable for my Sunday morning scholarship. Fewer young women were interested in becoming debutantes and fewer still seemed to think it was the sort of thing they wanted to list when they became engaged to be married. The announcements in the *Times* gradually came to include a broader slice of the population. An increasing number of the announcements seemed to include the information that the bride was going to retain what in times gone by had been referred to as her maiden name. For connoisseurs of wedding announcements, the bride's decision about her name was subject to further analysis. You had to wonder, I pointed out, whether the Nancy Barnes who announces that she will be keeping her surname after marrying a young man named Cholmondeley Rhoenheusch is a committed feminist or just a weak speller.

For a while, there was a fashion in hyphenating names. In 1976, I felt obliged to warn the public that if Penelope Shaughnessy married Nathaniel Underthaler, while her best friend, Jennifer Morgenwasser, married Jeremiah Christiansen, and then the children of those two unions, Jedediah Shaughnessy-Underthaler and Victoria Morgenwasser-Christiansen, themselves got married—a prospect that the two old friends, Penelope Shaughnessy-Underthaler and Jennifer Morgenwasser-Christiansen, so devoutly wished that they were nearly afraid to mention it at the luncheons they continued to have over the years, even though such luncheons irritated any number of restaurant proprietors who tried to jam one of those double-barreled names into the tiny space allotted in the reservation book—these offspring would end up as a couple named Jedediah and Victoria Shaughnessy-Underthaler-Morgenwasser-Christiansen. In 1992, I wrote a column about Jane Silverman and Michael Thomas Flaherty, two richly accomplished graduates of Harvard, Class of 1987, who had, on the day they were married, legally adopted the merged family name of Flaherman.

A few years later, the tide began to turn. Not long after the *Times* ran a piece about the increasing number of young women who were taking their new husbands' names, there was a piece reporting that debutante cotillions were again becoming popular. So were old-fashioned weddings, featuring the bride in a white gown and a passel of bridesmaids in gowns of some other color. No one knew precisely why these signs of a return to pre-sixties conventions had begun to show up. One theory was, in its simplest form, that a hankering for a traditional wedding was a natural result of young women seeing pictures that recorded the weddings of their parents in the early seventies. There is Dad in his Nehru jacket. There is Mom in what looks like a cast-off nightgown. There is some odd version of a clergyman—a man with a simpering smile and loony sideburns and a copy of *The Prophet* by Kahlil Gibran. Is that Granny knee-deep in the weeds at the edge of the forest? Studying the pictures, these young women may have figured that there had to be a better way to get married than that.

Did that mean that our daughters would want no part of Caxton Hall Registry Office? They had certainly seen the picture taken of us walking down the sidewalk in front of the building where we had closed the deal before Barry J. Digweed. It hadn't been in the newspaper—as I remember, some movie star was married on the same day at some other registry office—but the photographer, remarkably enough, had sent us a print. Given my longtime interest in weddings, I had naturally begun discussing the setting for our daughters' ceremonies when the girls were still relatively young—say, five or six. Why didn't I bring it up before then? I suppose there was a certain assumption that they would get married in the courtyard where they had served as scene-boosters for someone else's ceremonies. My assumption about the courtyard changed when Abigail was about ten and I began talking to her about the possibility of having at least the reception, if not the ceremony, at Tiro a Segno, an Italian-American social club on Macdougal Street, only a few blocks from our house.

I don't suppose there is anyone who has more of a blanket disregard for clubs than Alice, unless it's some completely unreconstructed veteran of the Red Guards who has survived by keeping his mouth shut in free-market China. She made an exception of Tiro from the start—even though, since she was neither male nor Italian, her application for membership would have been subject to an automatic double blackball before anyone even said hello. We began going there in the late sixties, not long after Abigail's birth, with our friend Wally Popolizio. Wally was practicing law in the Village then, in an office called Fazio & Popolizio, sharing with the American Accordion Association. It was on Eighth Street, over the Florsheim shoe store. What I remember best about the office is that it displayed a wooden model of the cart Wally's father used to deliver coal and ice after the Popolizios emigrated to Leroy Street from Basilicata, in the boot of Italy, around the turn of the century. Wally had been active in the political battles between the regulars and the reformers in the Village—even though he had the style of a regular, he was with the reformers—and he spent some time as the head of Community Planning Board Number Two. He was later, at one time or another, a partner in a Wall Street law firm with a name like Thatcher Baxter Hatcher (a firm Wally and I both referred to as "the goyim") and the chairman of the New York City Housing Authority. The wooden model of the ice cart accompanied him wherever he went. I met Wally on what he would have called "a real estate matter"—someone had recommended him as a lawyer who could provide guidance around the pitfalls involved in buying a place to live in the Village—and once the matter had been disposed of, he seemed to add to his other duties the informal responsibility of seeing to it that our family didn't do anything disastrously foolish. He did not relinquish that responsibility until his death, in 1992.

Wally had a strong sense of family. Once, when I seemed about to entangle myself in some small public contretemps, he phoned to tell me that whatever it was I wanted to say could be said later, when my enemies couldn't use it against me. "And who are your enemies?" he asked, as if conducting a review of examination questions with a particularly slow student.

I had been wondering about the same thing myself. "Enemies?" I said.

"Everybody but your family," he said, and hung up.

Alice loved Wally, but we didn't have to face the question of whether her affection for him would have been strong enough to overcome her feelings about clubs even if Tiro a Segno had resembled the sort of place that comes to mind when you think of, say, the Union League Club or the Racquets Club. Tiro, which had been put together out of two Village brownstones, didn't look like an uptown club. The dining room was dominated by a huge mural of the harbor of Naples which had been improved by the addition of some other famous sights of Italy, such as Pompeii and Michelangelo's David. The atmosphere was what I think of as New York Italian. I confessed a long time ago that I'm soft on Italians. I meant New York Italians—particularly lower Manhattan Italians—although it's also true that I often find myself in a sunny frame of mind when I'm in Italy. If I had to face a panel that told me it is out of bounds these days to express even affectionate opinions of people by ethnic groups, I could probably come up with a couple of lower Manhattan Italians I don't like, but my heart wouldn't be in it.

At Tiro, people seemed to stick to their own tables less than they might in an uptown club; Wally's friends often stopped to chat at our table, and sometimes sat down to join us for a double espresso. The food, of course, had nothing at all in common with the sort of club food that seems designed to reassure a guest that all members have descended from bona fide Puritans. A member of Tiro, setting aside his plate of roasted peppers to give the waiter room to put down the pasta e fagioli, might discuss standard American club food with a polite but slightly patronizing smile. Members of Tiro tended to take a strong, critical interest in what was served at the club. Wally told us that there had once been a ferocious controversy over a suggestion by one member that peanuts be included in the nut bowls at the bar—a suggestion that some other members believed would leave any respectable guest with the impression that Tiro a Segno had fallen into the hands of peasants or know-nothings.

"I happen to know that the Yale Club has peanuts at the bar," I said.

Wally shrugged and threw open his hands in a gesture that said, "Precisely my point. They don't know any better. Case closed."

I hadn't thought of Tiro in connection with the girls' weddings until someone who had stopped off at our table to say hello to Wally one day happened to mention that he had arranged for a friend to have a large anniversary party at the club. "I didn't know that nonmembers could have events here," I said, when Wally's friend had left. "You mean that, just to take an example, a member could arrange to have the wedding reception of a friend's daughter here?"

"Consider it done," Wally said.

What followed is probably a lesson in the advantages of waiting until your daughters are, say, in junior high school before committing yourself to a wedding reception venue. First, it was decided that Wally's acceptance of the Housing Authority job made it necessary for him to resign from Tiro a Segno, even though Tiro, as an ethnic organization, was actually exempt from the city administration's policy of not permitting its officials to belong to clubs that did not admit women members. I knew another member who could arrange the reception, but then some of the newer members decided that a redecoration of the clubhouse was long overdue. When I went to lunch at Tiro just after the renovation, the place was almost unrecognizable. The walls of the bar that I had remembered as having red flocked wallpaper were of a light-colored wood that I learned was bleached mahogany. The dining room was also redone in bleached mahogany. The lighting was recessed. The mural of Pompeii and David and the Bay of Naples was gone. Tiro still didn't look like an uptown club, but it looked something like the businessmen's luncheon clubs that are sometimes found on the top floor of office buildings in larger American cities. If you had to describe the look in one word, "understated" might come to mind. A lot of the members thought Tiro looked a lot more attractive, and I wouldn't want to argue with that; it's their club. But I knew it didn't look like the sort of place we'd had in mind for a wedding reception.

Tiro a Segno was replaced so naturally in my wedding reception thinking by Triple Eight Palace—a huge dim sum parlor on the second floor of a Chinese shopping mall under the Manhattan Bridge—that I can't remember the precise moment the decision was made. In the years we had been making our walks to Chinatown for lunch, a number of different dim sum restaurants got our patronage. We had brief flings with a couple of the flashy new barns that had become popular with the influx of prosperous Hong Kong immigrants who wouldn't have deigned to eat at the sort of Formica-table joints we used to frequent. For a while, we favored a run-down-looking place a couple of blocks from where Chinatown seemed to end — a place whose customers were an odd mixture of Chinese eating rather exotic dim sum and people who appeared to be city employees taking advantage of a $3.95 special lunch combination. Eventually, we found ourselves gravitating toward Triple Eight, one of the modern restaurants done in Hong Kong style. In addition to the usual dim-sum carts circling around, it customarily had two or three stands set up around the room where special items like clams were cooked to order. It took us a while to feel at home there. The restaurant occupies all of the mall's second floor; when you reach the top of the escalator, you can survey the entire domain of the Triple Eight, except for one large room entered through an archway. I got the idea that management tended to use the room through the archway to accommodate just about any Westerners who wandered in. Although I had to admit that there were plenty of Chinese in there, too, we referred to it as the Foreign Devils Room. After a couple of visits, we would explain to the greeter leading us toward the Foreign Devils Room that we'd prefer to sit out in the open with the other folks.

The Triple Eight people were accommodating about letting us sit wherever we wanted, which made me suspect that a policy of seating Occidentals in the Foreign Devils Room might have been a figment of my imagination. Once we were settled and relaxed in the main part of the restaurant, I began to notice that the Triple Eight Palace had a stage. It also had partitions that could be employed to carve out whatever portion of the vast space was needed. I wouldn't want to say that the Triple Eight's name, with its repetition of a number that is considered lucky by Chinese, was a large factor in its growing attraction in my mind as a wedding reception site, but someone with an acknowledged respect for the Evil Eye does not find such a name risible. "Abigail," I said one day, after a particularly satisfying order of vegetable dumplings, "I believe we might have found the place."

Naturally, details have been added over the years. Abigail occasionally comes up with menu suggestions, heavy on the hockey pucks and slime. At one point, she decided that we ought to try to hire the woman who occupies a tiny shed just off Mott Street and uses what looks like a musket-ball mold to produce what are called Hong Kong egg cakes—delicacies whose taste I once described as what madeleine would taste like if the French really understood such things. Sarah began saying that visits to the Triple Eight were causing her to reconsider her previous choice in wedding locales—one of the drive-through wedding palaces of Las Vegas. Our friend James Edmunds, from New Iberia, Louisiana, observed that, if we happened to want to hold the ceremony as well as the reception at the Triple Eight, having the bride and groom and their attendants emerge on the escalator as the loudspeaker from the karaoke bar below played the wedding march from *Lohengrin* would add a dramatic touch. I reminded Abigail that we could use the Foreign Devils Room for the people we absolutely had to have to the wedding but really didn't much like—the groom's family, perhaps.

Alice, I have to say, has not greeted these ideas with a tremendous amount of enthusiasm. It has occurred to me—and I say this without a hint of criticism—that Alice might prefer a venue that is a little more, well, traditional.

"Isn't it customary for the mother of the bride to have something to say about this?" she asked me one day.

"You mean you'd like to put in a word for those taro cakes they do so well on the griddle?" I replied. Alice is crazy about those taro cakes they do on the griddle.

Alice didn't say anything for a while. Then she said, "What if Abigail, for instance, ends up marrying someone who doesn't like the idea of having his wedding reception at a dim sum restaurant?"

"You mean a stiff?" I said. "Why would Abigail want to marry a stiff?"

16

Family, at Length

Not long after Sarah turned nineteen, it came to my attention that we could no longer be officially considered a traditional American family. According to the Census Bureau, I'd read somewhere, a traditional American family consists of two parents and one or more children under the age of eighteen. I wrote a column suggesting that the definition of a traditional American family be expanded — or, alternatively, that we be given a waiver. I said that it hardly seemed fair to lump us in with what comes to mind when you think of households that do not qualify as traditional American families — the ex-stepchild of someone's former marriage living with someone who is under the mistaken impression that she is the aunt of somebody or other, say, or a lot of unrelated people who have long, tangled hair and children named Sunshine. The Census Bureau did not reply. Ever since then, I've occasionally imagined myself in one of those casual conversations travelers used to fall into, often in the club car of a cross-country train, in movies of the forties. At one point, the other traveler says to me, "Are you a family man?" What am I supposed to say to that? "Well, although we don't technically have any children eighteen or under, quite often, particularly during the holiday season . . ."

It's true that younger children have the sort of impact on your life—an impact on where you go and what you eat and even how you talk—that reminds you constantly that you're a family. In that regard, I think of a telephone conversation I once had when Abigail was a year and a half or so and we were borrowing a friend's house in East Anglia. I was describing to another friend—an art historian whose kids were not far from Abigail's age—how simple it would be for her and her family to make a trip from London to see us. "The train passes through some beautiful country," I said. "I'm reliably informed by Abigail that moo-cows are plainly visible from the train window." As I went on with my description of the journey, my friend suddenly said, "Oh, my God!"

"What happened?" I asked.

"I was taking notes on the directions," she said. "And I wrote down 'moo-cows.' "

By the time Sarah turned nineteen, we had admittedly returned to our pre-children speech patterns and eating habits. Some years had passed since we'd said, "It might be easier just to stop at McDonald's." We admittedly had long stretches with no children around the house. But we had been assured by parents with more years in the game that we could absolutely count on the children returning eventually—to use the washer-dryer or the computer, if for no other reason. I took the position, in other words, that we were just as traditional as any

American family, just temporarily understaffed—like a hockey team that has a couple of guys in the penalty box but should still be thought of as a considerable presence on the ice. Several years later, in fact, when Abigail was in law school and living around the corner from us, we invited her to a small dinner we were having for an old friend whose book had just been published. She showed up early, in a dandy dinner-party costume, carrying a large bag. "I would like to say two things to you, Abigail," I said. "One is that you look particularly smashing tonight. The other is that I believe you're the only guest who has brought her laundry."

Since then, my mind has turned from time to time to what criteria you might use, other than the age of the youngest child, to register groups of related people as traditional American families. Language would be one. Virtually all families have words and phrases of their own—a phrase for describing some way of preparing a leftover potato dish that they all love, for instance, or a homemade word for the remote-control device used to change the channels on a television set (a device that is properly called a shmoudger, with the "ou" pronounced as in "would" or "could"). On that score, our family qualified as a traditional American family even after the girls left home. Among us, leaving a particularly dirty pot soaking in the sink overnight, either to loosen the grime or to put off the inevitable, is still called giving it a Suzie-soak, after a sweet au pair named Suzie, whose custom it was to wait until morning. Even after our household became whatever that long German word is for tuition-free, we continued to call any fee-producing speech I gave a "tuition gig." We never stopped using a phrase we'd heard originally from our friend Danny Jowell, who, at about the time he was playing the robber with the foxlike grin, referred to all grown-ups as "big faces." (He also referred to many of them as "nin-compoop twits," but that's another story.) When Sarah was in sixth or seventh grade, a school friend whose father was a dentist happened to be visiting one day while Sarah was entertaining us with the laborious instructions a neighbor of ours gave baby-sitters on how to talk to her children in a way that bolstered their self-esteem.

"But she's right," Sarah's friend said. "Otherwise you could mess up their little cavities."

"Little cavities?" Alice asked.

"You know," Sarah's friend said. "People have little cavities in their heads, and it's real easy to mess them up." We continue to refer to the psyche as the little cavity, as in "I don't know how they made it to Parrsboro, because he is strictly guts and throwup and her little cavity is messed up beyond repair."

As it happens, some of our family language was developed only as the girls approached the age that would disqualify us as a traditional family in the view of the Census Bureau. When Abigail was a teenager, she was in some summer program while Alice and Sarah and I were off somewhere, and my postcards to her began including references to someone called TM. It seemed to me that Abigail was getting a bit old for me to be writing her something like "Mommy has bought remarkably little so far," and I always thought "your mother" sounded like what a corporate lawyer might say to his son when they're having a conversation in the lawyer's study, in reference to someone the lawyer barely knows. ("Your mother thinks you should go to boarding school, and, given the way you performed last semester at Hadley Country Day, I believe that's a sound idea.") Abigail did not have to be told what TM stood for; it obviously meant The Mother. In the years after we began referring to Alice as TM, we also added, among other words and phrases, the word "Kerensky" to mean a young man one of the girls was seeing who did not seem destined to become a permanent addition to our family. This was an allusion to Alexander Kerensky, the social democrat who was the post-revolutionary Premier of Russia until the Bolsheviks shoved him aside—historically, a transitional figure. We might say of some pleasant enough young fellow, "He's a nice boy, but a Kerensky."

I would admit to the Census Bureau that the girls don't exactly live at home. I might even admit that, having moved an exercise bike into Abigail's room at one point, I began referring to it as "the gym." I would admit that I've told even Sarah—the baby—that she has "many attributes of a grown-up." I would admit that, now that we can't be counted on to be having a family dinner together, the Gray Line would not think of us as a dependable stop for showing a nuclear family in lower Manhattan. But does that mean that we're no longer traditional? Abigail's messages on our answering machine often begin "Hi, big faces." Is it really true that a family—a traditional American family—can't have two sets of big faces?

I thought about these matters when Abigail and I took that trip to Veracruz together. I had wanted to go to Veracruz for years. From somewhere, maybe a movie whose title I mixed up with another movie, I'd formed a picture—an incorrect picture, as it turned out—of what I thought Veracruz would be like: In a bar with peeling paint, next to the docks, a man who looks as if he shaves at night so he'll look tough all the next day is talking to an equally sinister-looking man about arranging a shipment of something that doesn't bear talking about to a country where customs officials tend to be grateful for small gifts. Above them, a rusty ceiling fan goes "pahCHUCKetuh, pahCHUCKetuh, pahCHUCKetuh . . ."

Although this may not sound like a vision likely to attract the average tourist, Abigail, who was then living in California, had said that she'd love to go along. Abigail shares my taste for sitting in squares—although, as it happens, she also shares Alice's taste for taking a tour of, say, the Palladian villas of the Veneto. Alice and I had traveled a lot with our daughters during what I used to call the family-travel window of opportunity— the years when the kids are old enough to travel reasonably comfortably with their parents but not so old that they have better things to do. Given my inability to envision them at another age, I suppose it never occurred to me that they would be available again in the years after college, willing to indulge a father's daydreams. I realized that in rearing children we had also been training traveling companions.

A traveling companion trained by our family would be comfortable hanging around. In Veracruz, Abigail and I would while away an evening at a café on what is, to my mind, just about the perfect Mexican central square—with a beautifully maintained park in the middle and a splendid cathedral on one side and a plentiful supply of the ornate iron benches (painted green, with the crest of the republic in the middle) that I have always considered one of Mexico's great gifts to civilized living. I would dwell on my principal theory of Mexican music. That sort of thing—unloading theories—is a father's role. Why should it end when the captive breakfast audience gets liberated? I told Abigail that when I first went to Mexico, many years before, I used to offer ten pesos to anyone who had ever heard an entire Mexican song that didn't contain the word corazón—the Spanish word for heart— at least once. Since the exchange rate as Abigail and I spoke was something like three thousand pesos to a dollar, I resisted the temptation to add, "And I'm talking about the days when ten pesos was ten pesos."

We happened to be in the perfect place to propound theories on Mexican music to your daughter. Even on the quietest of evenings in the central square of Veracruz, a visitor who is at all alert to his surroundings can be assured of hearing, at the same time, three or four marimba bands, a couple of Mexican cowboy combos, an itinerant whistle salesman demonstrating his wares, a band playing for the accompaniment of the couples who are doing the *danzón* in front of City Hall, and at least one traditional Veracruzana trio of two guitarists and a harpist, who, for a small consideration, will sing a song he makes up on the spot to your specifications. When, after thinking over the investment for a few evenings, we finally decided to pop for the customized song from the Veracruzana harpist, Abigail said, "How about asking him to do a song about a Mexican songwriter trying to write a song that does not have the word *corazón* in it?"

"Abigail," I said, "whoever brought you up did a terrific job."

Maybe the Census Bureau could, while greatly expanding the definition of a traditional American family, create sub-categories based on the stage the family is in. I wouldn't object to that. I'm perfectly willing to acknowledge that sitting in the central square of Veracruz, watching Abigail explain in a confident Spanish to a puzzled Veracruzana harpist exactly what we'd like for him to do, is a far cry from watching her and Sarah as little girls, changed into their pajamas on a night flight to London and ready to curl up with their teddy bears and go to sleep. I would argue, though, that we're simply a traditional American family at a different stage.

I'm willing to take notice — and maybe even file a form with

the Census Bureau—when a stage passes. For a number of
years, high school friends in Kansas City who were trying to be
understanding about my bizarre decision to live in New York
would say, "I guess the cultural opportunities must be wonder-
ful," and I would always answer, "Well, we see a lot of school
plays." By then, Alice's policy on attending school plays (a policy that also covered pageants, talent shows, reviews, recitals and
spring assemblies) was well known. She believes that if your
child is in a school play and you don't go to every performance,
including the special Thursday matinee for the fourth grade,
the county will come and take the child. Anyone who has lived
for some years in a house where that policy is strictly observed
may have fleeting moments of envy toward people who have
seen only one or two productions of *Our Town*.

At one point, though, we both had to face the fact that the
school play phase was passing. As we walked into an auditorium
and were handed a program filled with the usual jokey résumés
of the participants and cheerful ads from well-wishers, I realized
that this would be our last opportunity to see one of our children perform in a school theatrical event. That view was based
partly on the fact that the child in question was twenty-six years
old. She was about to graduate from law school. I was assuming
that the JDs slogging through the bar-exam cram course would
not decide to break the tedium with, say, a production of *Anything Goes*.

As I waited for the curtain to go up on the 1995 New York
University Law Revue, entitled *The Lawrank Redemption*, I
found myself thinking back on our life as parental playgoers. I
realized that I couldn't recall seeing either of our daughters in
one of those classic nursery school pageant roles as an angel or
a rabbit or an eggplant. I thought I might be experiencing a

failure of memory—another occasion for one of my daughters to say, as gently as possible, "Pop, you're losing it"—but they later confirmed that their nursery school was undramatic, except on those occasions when a particularly flamboyant hair-puller was pushing the "words not hands, dear" policy to its limits.

I did recall seeing one or another of them as an Indian in *Peter Pan* and as the judge in *Trial by Jury* and as Nancy in *Oliver!* and as the narrator (unpersuasively costumed as a motorcycle tough) in *Joseph and the Amazing Technicolor Dream Coat* and as a gondolier in *The Gondoliers*. We'd heard their voices in a lot of songs, even if a number of other kids were sometimes singing at the same time. We had heard "Dites-moi, Pourquoi" sung sweetly and "Don't Tell Mama" belted out. All and all, we'd had a pretty good run.

I don't want to appear to be one of those parents who doze through the show unless their own kids are in the spotlight. When I hear "Singular Sensation" from *Chorus Line*, I can still see Julia Greenberg's little brother, Daniel, doing a slow, almost stately tap-dance interpretation in high-topped quite tapless sneakers. I'm not even certain what my own girls did in the school talent show at PS 3 which I remember mainly for the performance of the three Korn brothers. One of the Korns worked furiously on the Rubik's Cube while his older brother accompanied him on the piano. The youngest brother, who must have been six or seven, occasionally held up signs that said something like "Two Sides to Go" or "One Side to Go." I have always had a weakness for family acts.

I won't pretend that all school performances were unalloyed joy. We used to go every year to watch our girls tap-dance in a recital that also included gymnastics, and the gymnastics instructor was an earnest man who seemed intent on guarding against the possibility of anyone's getting through the evening without a thorough understanding of what goes into a simple somersault. He described each demonstration in such excruciating detail that I used to pass the time trying to imagine him helplessly tangled in his own limbs as the result of a simple somersault that had gone terribly wrong:

"Untie me," he is saying.

"Not until you take an oath of silence," I reply.

Even so, I came to believe over the years that Alice's policy on school plays, which sounds extreme, actually makes sense. On some occasions when I'm asked for child-rearing advice from young couples, I find myself deviating just a bit from my standard answer of "Try to get one that doesn't spit up." I finally figured that it was O.K. to remind them—this was a reminder, not a piece of advice—that a school play was more important than anything else they might have had scheduled for that evening. I realized that school plays were invented partly to give parents an easy opportunity to demonstrate their priorities. If they can get off work for the Thursday matinee, I tell them, all the better.